thanks...

Shortly after **Detecting Women** made its debut in January 1995, we started getting letters, phone calls, faxes and e-mail insisting we publish a pocket guide. We followed your advice and take great pleasure in introducing the **Detecting Women 2 Pocket Guide**.

To those of you who sent comments, encouragement, suggestions and support, we offer our warmest thanks, with regret that we were not able to acknowledge each of you personally. You kept us busy carrying out your orders, and this one's for you!

We hope this pocket guide meets with your approval and we look forward to hearing from you again. We know you'll have more ideas for sharing the joy of reading mysteries.

Willetta

Purple Moon Press
Dearborn, Michigan, USA
fax 313-593-4087
<nrgx40a@prodigy.com>

Pocket Guidelines...

This Pocket Guide is designed as a companion to the full-size edition of **Detecting Women 2**. Owing to the pocket guide's small size, it includes "just the facts"—author name (last name first), character name and book titles in correct series order.

Whenever an author is writing under a pseudonym, you'll find a 🅿 after that name. The author's true identity is cross-referenced in the Pseudonyms chapter of the full-size edition of **Detecting Women 2**.

Dates of publication appear in two-digit format ('95 = 1995) based on the earliest date of publication (not necessarily the U.S. date). For alternate titles, "U.S." and "Britain" indicate country of publication, while "APA" denotes "also published as."

Starred titles identify mystery award winners and nominees. Solid stars are used for winners and open stars for nominees. In the big book, the specific awards are also listed. Because mystery awards are a fairly recent phenomenon, you should not overlook titles from earlier eras.

Two columns of check boxes are provided to record books you own and books you've read, or to keep score and rate your favorites. We've been told that even those couples who read together prefer to "check" separately, so this format will permit them to share the checkbook, so to speak. Whatever your reason for wanting two sets of boxes, they're here.

The Master List in the full-size edition includes author profiles, character descriptions and series settings, along with complete indexes by mystery type, series setting, character name and pseudonym (some of which will surprise you).

Along with an extensive bibliography, glossary and master index, the big book includes a short story grid featuring 24 major anthologies, allowing you to locate the stories written by your favorite authors.

Rounding out the full-size edition are complete lists of all 3,495 series titles in two formats—by year of publication and alphabetical order. Both lists identify award winners and the first book in a series. The chronological section also includes some interesting charts showing the recent explosion of series titles written by women. You won't want to miss it.

Test your mystery trivia skills

Scattered throughout these pages are questions to test your knowledge of mysteries written by women. Answers are printed inside the back cover (behind the notepad). These are just a sample of what you'll learn in **Detecting Women 2**.

A

ADAMS, Deborah
Jesus Creek, Tennessee
- ❑ ❑ 1 - All the Great Pretenders ('92) ☆
- ❑ ❑ 2 - All the Crazy Winters ('92)
- ❑ ❑ 3 - All the Dark Disguises ('93)
- ❑ ❑ 4 - All the Hungry Mothers ('93)
- ❑ ❑ 5 - All the Deadly Beloved ('95)

ADAMSON, M. J. (Mary Jo)
Balthazar Marten & Sixto Cardenas
- ❑ ❑ 1 - Not Till a Hot January ('87)
- ❑ ❑ 2 - A February Face ('87)
- ❑ ❑ 3 - Remember March ('88)
- ❑ ❑ 4 - April When They Woo ('88)
- ❑ ❑ 5 - May's Newfangled Mirth ('89)

AIRD, Catherine 🄿
Christopher Dennis "Seedy" Sloan
- ❑ ❑ 1 - The Religious Body ('66)
- ❑ ❑ 2 - Henrietta Who? ('68)
- ❑ ❑ 3 - The Complete Steel ('69)
      [U.S.-The Stately Home Murder]
- ❑ ❑ 4 - A Late Phoenix ('70)
- ❑ ❑ 5 - His Burial Too ('73)
- ❑ ❑ 6 - Slight Mourning ('75)
- ❑ ❑ 7 - Parting Breath ('77)
- ❑ ❑ 8 - Some Die Eloquent ('79)
- ❑ ❑ 9 - Passing Strange ('80)
- ❑ ❑ 10 - Last Respects ('82)
- ❑ ❑ 11 - A Dead Liberty ('87)
- ❑ ❑ 12 - A Going Concern ('93)

ALBERT, Susan Wittig
China Bayles
- ❑ ❑ 1 - Thyme of Death ('92) ☆ ☆
- ❑ ❑ 2 - Witches' Bane ('93)
- ❑ ❑ 3 - Hangman's Root ('94)
- ❑ ❑ 4 - Rosemary Remembered ('95)

ALLEN, Irene 🄿
Elizabeth Elliot
- ❑ ❑ 1 - Quaker Silence ('92)
- ❑ ❑ 2 - Quaker Witness ('93)

ALLEN, Kate 🄿

Alison Kaine
☐ ☐ 1 - Tell Me What You Like ('93)
☐ ☐ 2 - Give My Secrets Back ('95)

ALLINGHAM, Margery

Albert Campion
☐ ☐ 1 - The Crime at Black Dudley ('29)
      [U.S.-The Black Dudley Murder]
☐ ☐ 2 - Mystery Mile ('30)
☐ ☐ 3 - Look to the Lady ('31)
      [U.S.-The Gryth Chalice Mystery]
☐ ☐ 4 - Police at the Funeral ('31)
☐ ☐ 5 - Sweet Danger ('33)
      [U.S.-Kingdom of Death]
      [APA-The Fear Sign]
☐ ☐ 6 - Death of a Ghost ('34)
☐ ☐ 7 - Flowers for the Judge ('36)
      [APA-Legacy in Blood]
☐ ☐ 8 - Dancers in Mourning ('37)
      [APA-Who Killed Chloe?]
☐ ☐ 9 - The Case of the Late Pig ('37)
☐ ☐ 10 - The Fashion in Shrouds ('38)
☐ ☐ 11 - Traitor's Purse ('41)
      [APA-The Sabotage Murder Mystery]
☐ ☐ 12 - Coroner's Pidgin ('45)
      [U.S.-Pearls Before Swine]
☐ ☐ 13 - More Work for the Undertaker ('49)
☐ ☐ 14 - The Tiger in the Smoke ('52)
☐ ☐ 15 - No Love Lost ('54)
☐ ☐ 16 - The Beckoning Lady ('55)
      [U.S.-The Estate of the Beckoning Lady]
☐ ☐ 17 - Hide My Eyes ('58) ★
      [U.S.-Tether's End] [APA-Ten Were Missing]
☐ ☐ 18 - The China Governess ('62)
☐ ☐ 19 - The Mind Readers ('65)
☐ ☐ 20 - Cargo of Eagles ('68) [with P. Y. Carter]
☐ ☐ 21 - Mr. Campion's Farthing ('69) [by P. Y. Carter]
☐ ☐ 22 - Mr. Campion's Falcon ('70) [by P. Y. Carter]
      [U.S.-Mr. Campion's Quarry]

AMEY, Linda

Blair Emerson
☐ ☐ 1 - Bury Her Sweetly ('92)
☐ ☐ 2 - At Dead of Night ('95)

ANDREAE, Christine
Lee Squires
- ❑ ❑ 1 - Trail of Murder ('92) ☆
- ❑ ❑ 2 - Grizzly, A Murder ('94)

ANDREWS, Sarah
Em Hansen
- ❑ ❑ 1 - Tensleep ('94)
- ❑ ❑ 2 - A Fall in Denver ('95)

ARMSTRONG, Charlotte
MacDougal Duff
- ❑ ❑ 1 - Lay on, Mac Duff! ('42)
- ❑ ❑ 2 - The Case of the Weird Sisters ('43)
- ❑ ❑ 3 - The Innocent Flower ('45)

ARNOLD, Margot 🄿
Penny Spring & Sir Toby Glendower
- ❑ ❑ 1 - Exit Actors, Dying ('79)
- ❑ ❑ 2 - Zadock's Treasure ('79)
- ❑ ❑ 3 - The Cape Cod Caper ('80)
- ❑ ❑ 4 - Death of a Voodoo Doll ('82)
- ❑ ❑ 5 - Lament for a Lady Laird ('82)
- ❑ ❑ 6 - Death on a Dragon's Tongue ('82)
- ❑ ❑ 7 - The Menehune Murders ('89)
- ❑ ❑ 8 - Toby's Folly ('90)
- ❑ ❑ 9 - The Catacomb Conspiracy ('91)
- ❑ ❑ 10 - Cape Cod Conundrum ('92)
- ❑ ❑ 11 - Dirge for a Dorset Druid ('94)
- ❑ ❑ 12 - The Midas Murders ('95)

ATHERTON, Nancy
Aunt Dimity
- ❑ ❑ 1 - Aunt Dimity's Death ('92)
- ❑ ❑ 2 - Aunt Dimity and the Duke ('94)
- ❑ ❑ 3 - Aunt Dimity's Good Deed ('96)

AYRES, Noreen
Samantha "Smokey" Brandon
- ❑ ❑ 1 - A World the Color of Salt ('92)
- ❑ ❑ 2 - Carcass Trade ('94)
- ❑ ❑ 3 - The Long Slow Whistle of the Moon ('96)

B

BABBIN, Jacqueline
Clovis Kelly
❑ ❑ 1 - Prime Time Corpse ('72)
    [APA–Bloody Special ('89)]
❑ ❑ 2 - Bloody Soaps ('89)

BABSON, Marian
Douglas Perkins
❑ ❑ 1 - Cover-up Story ('71)
❑ ❑ 2 - Murder on Show ('72)
    [U.S.-Murder at the Cat Show]
❑ ❑ 3 - Tourists are for Trapping ('89)
❑ ❑ 4 - In the Teeth of Adversity ('90)
Eve Sinclair & Trixie Dolan
❑ ❑ 1 - Reel Murder ('86)
❑ ❑ 2 - Encore Murder ('89)
❑ ❑ 3 - Shadows in Their Blood ('93)

BAKER, Nikki 🄿
Virginia Kelly
❑ ❑ 1 - In the Game ('91)
❑ ❑ 2 - The Lavender House Murder ('92)
❑ ❑ 3 - Long Goodbyes ('93)

BALLARD, Mignon
Eliza Figg
❑ ❑ 1 - Minerva Cries Murder ('93)

BANKS, Carolyn
Robin Vaughn
❑ ❑ 1 - Death by Dressage ('93)
❑ ❑ 2 - Groomed for Death ('94)
❑ ❑ 3 - Murder Well-Bred ('95)

BANNISTER, Jo
Dr. Clio Rees & Harry Marsh
❑ ❑ 1 - Striving with Gods ('84)
❑ ❑ 2 - Gilgamesh ('89)
❑ ❑ 3 - The Going Down of the Sun ('90)

Frank Shapiro, Cal Donovan & Liz Graham
- ❏ ❏ 1 - A Bleeding of Innocents ('93)
- ❏ ❏ 2 - Charisma ('94)
  [Britain-Sins of the Heart]
- ❏ ❏ 3 - A Taste for Burning ('95)
  [Britain-Burning Desires]

BARBER, Willetta Ann
Christopher "Kit" Storm
- ❏ ❏ 1 - Murder Draws a Line ('40)
- ❏ ❏ 2 - Pencil Points to Murder ('41)
- ❏ ❏ 3 - Drawn Conclusion ('42)
- ❏ ❏ 4 - Murder Enters the Picture ('42)
- ❏ ❏ 5 - The Noose Is Drawn ('45)
- ❏ ❏ 6 - Drawback to Murder ('47)
- ❏ ❏ 7 - The Deed Is Drawn ('49)

BARNES, Linda
Carlotta Carlyle
- ❏ ❏ 1 - A Trouble of Fools ('87) ★ ☆ ☆
- ❏ ❏ 2 - The Snake Tattoo ('89)
- ❏ ❏ 3 - Coyote ('90)
- ❏ ❏ 4 - Steel Guitar ('91)
- ❏ ❏ 5 - Snapshot ('93)
- ❏ ❏ 6 - Hardware ('95)
Michael Spraggue III
- ❏ ❏ 1 - Blood Will Have Blood ('82)
- ❏ ❏ 2 - Bitter Finish ('83)
- ❏ ❏ 3 - Dead Heat ('84)
- ❏ ❏ 4 - Cities of the Dead ('86)

BARR, Nevada
Anna Pigeon
- ❏ ❏ 1 - Track of the Cat ('93) ★ ★
- ❏ ❏ 2 - A Superior Death ('94)
- ❏ ❏ 3 - Ill Wind ('95)
- ❏ ❏ 4 - Fire Storm ('96)

BEATON, M. C. 🅿
Agatha Raisin
- ❏ ❏ 1 - Agatha Raisin and the Quiche of Death ('92)
- ❏ ❏ 2 - Agatha Raisin and the Vicious Vet ('93)
- ❏ ❏ 3 - Agatha Raisin and the Potted Gardener ('94)
- ❏ ❏ 4 - Agatha Raisin and the Walkers of Dembley ('95)

Hamish Macbeth

- ☐ ☐ 1 - Death of a Gossip ('85)
- ☐ ☐ 2 - Death of a Cad ('87)
- ☐ ☐ 3 - Death of an Outsider ('88)
- ☐ ☐ 4 - Death of a Perfect Wife ('89)
- ☐ ☐ 5 - Death of a Hussy ('90)
- ☐ ☐ 6 - Death of a Snob ('91)
- ☐ ☐ 7 - Death of a Prankster ('92)
- ☐ ☐ 8 - Death of a Glutton ('93)
- ☐ ☐ 9 - Death of a Travelling Man ('93)
- ☐ ☐ 10 - Death of a Charming Man ('94)
- ☐ ☐ 11 - Death of a Nag ('95)

BECK, K. K. ℗

Iris Cooper

- ☐ ☐ 1 - Death in a Deck Chair ('84)
- ☐ ☐ 2 - Murder in a Mummy Case ('85)
- ☐ ☐ 3 - Peril Under the Palms ('89)

Jane da Silva

- ☐ ☐ 1 - A Hopeless Case ('92)
- ☐ ☐ 2 - Amateur Night ('93)
- ☐ ☐ 3 - Electric City ('94)
- ☐ ☐ 4 - Cold Smoked ('95)

BEDFORD, Jean

Anna Southwood

- ☐ ☐ 1 - To Make a Killing ('90)
- ☐ ☐ 2 - Worse Than Death ('92)
- ☐ ☐ 3 - Signs of Murder ('93)

BEECHAM, Rose

Amanda Valentine

- ☐ ☐ 1 - Introducing Amanda Valentine ('92)
- ☐ ☐ 2 - Second Guess ('94)

BELFORT, Sophie ℗

Molly Rafferty

- ☐ ☐ 1 - The Lace Curtain Murders ('86)
- ☐ ☐ 2 - The Marvell College Murders ('91)
- ☐ ☐ 3 - Eyewitness to Murder ('92)

BELL, Josephine ℗

Amy Tupper

- ☐ ☐ 1 - Wolf! Wolf! ('79)
- ☐ ☐ 2 - A Question of Inheritance ('80)

Claude Warrington-Reeve
- ❏ ❏ 1 - Easy Prey ('59)
- ❏ ❏ 2 - A Well-Known Face ('60)
- ❏ ❏ 3 - A Flat Tire in Fulham ('63)
  [U.S.-Fiasco in Fulham]
  [APA–Room for a Body]

Dr. David Wintringham
- ❏ ❏ 1 - Murder in Hospital ('37)
- ❏ ❏ 2 - Death on the Borough Council ('37)
- ❏ ❏ 3 - Fall Over Cliff ('38)
- ❏ ❏ 4 - Death at Half-Term ('39)
  [APA–Curtain Call for a Corpse]
- ❏ ❏ 5 - From Natural Causes ('39)
- ❏ ❏ 6 - All Is Vanity ('40)
- ❏ ❏ 7 - Death at the Medical Board ('44)
- ❏ ❏ 8 - Death in Clairvoyance ('49)
- ❏ ❏ 9 - The Summer School Mystery ('50)
- ❏ ❏ 10 - Bones in the Barrow ('53)
- ❏ ❏ 11 - Fires at Fairlawn ('54)
- ❏ ❏ 12 - Death in Retirement ('56)
- ❏ ❏ 13 - The China Roundabout ('56)
  [U.S.-Murder on the Merry-Go-Round]
- ❏ ❏ 14 - The Seeing Eye ('58)

Dr. Henry Frost
- ❏ ❏ 1 - The Upfold Witch ('64)
- ❏ ❏ 2 - Death on the Reserve ('66)

Steven Mitchell
- ❏ ❏ 1 - The Port of London ('38)

BENNETT, Liza
Peg Goodenough
- ❏ ❏ 1 - Madison Avenue Murder ('89)
- ❏ ❏ 2 - Seventh Avenue Murder ('90)

BERENSON, Laurien
Gwen Harding
- ❏ ❏ 1 - Deep Cover ('94)

Melanie Travis
- ❏ ❏ 1 - A Pedigree to Die For ('95)
- ❏ ❏ 2 - Underdog ('96)

 What woman was once the highest paid writer in America and the first mystery author to make the best seller list?

BERRY, Carole
Bonnie Indermill
- ❑ ❑ 1 - The Letter of the Law ('87)
- ❑ ❑ 2 - The Year of the Monkey ('88)
- ❑ ❑ 3 - Good Night, Sweet Prince ('90)
- ❑ ❑ 4 - Island Girl ('91)
- ❑ ❑ 5 - The Death of a Difficult Woman ('94)

BISHOP, Claudia 🄿
Sarah & Meg Quilliam
- ❑ ❑ 1 - A Taste for Murder ('94)
- ❑ ❑ 2 - A Dash of Death ('95)
- ❑ ❑ 3 - A Pinch of Poison ('95)
- ❑ ❑ 4 - Murder Well-Done ('96)

BLACK, Veronica 🄿
Sister Joan
- ❑ ❑ 1 - A Vow of Silence ('90)
- ❑ ❑ 2 - A Vow of Chastity ('92)
- ❑ ❑ 3 - A Vow of Sanctity ('93)
- ❑ ❑ 4 - A Vow of Obedience ('93)
- ❑ ❑ 5 - A Vow of Penance ('94)
- ❑ ❑ 6 - A Vow of Devotion ('94)

BLACKMUR, L. L. 🄿
Galen Shaw & Julian Baugh
- ❑ ❑ 1 - Love Lies Slain ('89)
- ❑ ❑ 2 - Love Lies Bleeding ('89)

BLAND, Eleanor Taylor
Marti MacAlister
- ❑ ❑ 1 - Dead Time ('92)
- ❑ ❑ 2 - Slow Burn ('93)
- ❑ ❑ 3 - Gone Quiet ('94)
- ❑ ❑ 4 - Done Wrong ('95)

BLOCK, Barbara
Robin Light
- ❑ ❑ 1 - Chutes and Adders ('94)
- ❑ ❑ 2 - Twister ('94)

BORTHWICK, J. S. 🄿
Sarah Deane & Dr. Alex McKenzie
- ❑ ❑ 1 - The Case of the Hook-Billed Kites ('82)
- ❑ ❑ 2 - The Down East Murders ('85)
- ❑ ❑ 3 - The Student Body ('86)

❑ ❑ 4 - Bodies of Water ('90)
❑ ❑ 5 - Dude on Arrival ('92)
❑ ❑ 6 - The Bridled Groom ('94)
❑ ❑ 7 - Dolly Is Dead ('95)

BORTON, D. B. 🅿

Cat Caliban
❑ ❑ 1 - One for the Money ('93)
❑ ❑ 2 - Two Points for Murder ('93)
❑ ❑ 3 - Three Is a Crowd ('94)
❑ ❑ 4 - Four Elements of Murder ('95)
❑ ❑ 5 - Five Alarm Fire ('96)

BOWEN, Gail

Joanne Kilbourn
❑ ❑ 1 - Deadly Appearances ('90)
❑ ❑ 2 - Love and Murder ('91)
      [APA–Murder at the Mendel]
❑ ❑ 3 - The Wandering Soul Murders ('93)
❑ ❑ 4 - A Colder Kind of Death ('94) ★

BOWERS, Elisabeth

Meg Lacey
❑ ❑ 1 - Ladies' Night ('88)
❑ ❑ 2 - No Forwarding Address ('91)

BOYLAN, Eleanor

Clara Gamadge
❑ ❑ 1 - Working Murder ('89) ☆
❑ ❑ 2 - Murder Observed ('90)
❑ ❑ 3 - Murder Machree ('92)
❑ ❑ 4 - Pushing Murder ('93)

BRADLEY, Lynn

Coleman January
❑ ❑ 1 - Stand-in for Murder ('94)

BRAND, Christianna 🅿

Insp. Cockrill
❑ ❑ 1 - Heads You Lose ('41)
❑ ❑ 2 - Green for Danger ('44)
❑ ❑ 3 - Suddenly at his Residence ('46)
      [U.S.-The Crooked Wreath]
❑ ❑ 4 - Death of a Jezebel ('48)
❑ ❑ 5 - London Particular ('53) [U.S.-Fog of Doubt]
❑ ❑ 6 - Tour de Force ('55)

BRAUN, Lilian Jackson
Jim Qwilleran, Koko & Yum Yum
- ❏ ❏ 1 - The Cat Who Could Read Backwards ('66)
- ❏ ❏ 2 - The Cat Who Ate Danish Modern ('67)
- ❏ ❏ 3 - The Cat Who Turned On and Off ('68)
- ❏ ❏ 4 - The Cat Who Saw Red ('86) ☆
- ❏ ❏ 5 - The Cat Who Played Brahms ('87) ☆
- ❏ ❏ 6 - The Cat Who Played Post Office ('87)
- ❏ ❏ 7 - The Cat Who Knew Shakespeare ('88)
- ❏ ❏ 8 - The Cat Who Sniffed Glue ('88)
- ❏ ❏ 9 - The Cat Who Went Underground ('89)
- ❏ ❏ 10 - The Cat Who Talked to Ghosts ('90)
- ❏ ❏ 11 - The Cat Who Lived High ('90)
- ❏ ❏ 12 - The Cat Who Knew a Cardinal ('91)
- ❏ ❏ 13 - The Cat Who Moved a Mountain ('92)
- ❏ ❏ 14 - The Cat Who Wasn't There ('93)
- ❏ ❏ 15 - The Cat Who Came to Breakfast ('94)
- ❏ ❏ 16 - The Cat Who Went into the Closet ('94)
- ❏ ❏ 17 - The Cat Who Blew the Whistle ('95)
- ❏ ❏ 18 - The Cat Who Said Cheese ('96)

BRENNAN, Carol
Emily Silver
- ❏ ❏ 1 - In the Dark ('94)
- ❏ ❏ 2 - Chill of Summer ('95)
Liz Wareham
- ❏ ❏ 1 - Headhunt ('91)
- ❏ ❏ 2 - Full Commission ('92)

BRIDGE, Ann 🄿
Julia Probyn Jamieson
- ❏ ❏ 1 - The Lighthearted Quest ('56)
- ❏ ❏ 2 - The Portuguese Escape ('58)
- ❏ ❏ 3 - The Numbered Account ('60)
- ❏ ❏ 4 - The Dangerous Islands ('63)
- ❏ ❏ 5 - Emergency in the Pyrenees ('65)
- ❏ ❏ 6 - The Episode at Toledo ('66)
- ❏ ❏ 7 - The Malady in Madeira ('69)

BRIGHTWELL, Emily 🄿
Insp. Witherspoon & Mrs. Jeffries
- ❏ ❏ 1 - The Inspector and Mrs. Jeffries ('93)
- ❏ ❏ 2 - Mrs. Jeffries Dusts for Clues ('93)
- ❏ ❏ 3 - The Ghost and Mrs. Jeffries ('93)
- ❏ ❏ 4 - Mrs. Jeffries Takes Stock ('94)

❑ ❑ 5 - Mrs. Jeffries on the Ball ('94)
❑ ❑ 6 - Mrs. Jeffries on the Trail ('95)

BRILL, Toni 🄿
Midge Cohen
❑ ❑ 1 - Date with a Dead Doctor ('91)
❑ ❑ 2 - Date with a Plummeting Publisher ('93)

BROD, D. C.
Quint McCauley
❑ ❑ 1 - Murder in Store ('89)
❑ ❑ 2 - Error in Judgment ('90)
❑ ❑ 3 - Masquerade in Blue ('91)
      [APA-Framed in Blue]
❑ ❑ 4 - Brothers in Blood ('93)

BROWN, Lizbie 🄿
Elizabeth Blair
❑ ❑ 1 - Broken Star ('92)
❑ ❑ 2 - Turkey Tracks ('94)

BROWN, Rita Mae
Mary Minor Haristeen
❑ ❑ 1 - Wish You Were Here ('90)
❑ ❑ 2 - Rest in Pieces ('92)
❑ ❑ 3 - Murder at Monticello ('94)
❑ ❑ 4 - Pay Dirt ('95)

BUCHANAN, Edna
Britt Montero
❑ ❑ 1 - Contents Under Pressure ('92)
❑ ❑ 2 - Miami, It's Murder ('94) ☆
❑ ❑ 3 - Suitable for Framing ('95)
❑ ❑ 4 - Act of Betrayal ('96)

BUCKSTAFF, Kathryn
Morgana Dalton
❑ ❑ 1 - No One Dies in Branson ('94)

BURDEN, Pat
Henry Bassett
❑ ❑ 1 - Screaming Bones ('90) ☆
❑ ❑ 2 - Wreath of Honesty ('90)
❑ ❑ 3 - Bury Him Kindly ('92)
❑ ❑ 4 - Father, Forgive Me ('93)

BURKE, Jan
Irene Kelly
- ❏ ❏ 1 - Goodnight, Irene ('93) ☆ ☆
- ❏ ❏ 2 - Sweet Dreams, Irene ('94)
- ❏ ❏ 3 - Dear Irene, ('95)
- ❏ ❏ 4 - Remember Me, Irene ('96)

BURTON, Anne ℗
Richard Trenton
- ❏ ❏ 1 - The Dear Departed ('80)
- ❏ ❏ 2 - Where There's a Will ('80)
- ❏ ❏ 3 - Worse Than a Crime ('81)

BUSHELL, Agnes
Wilson & Wilder
- ❏ ❏ 1 - Shadowdance ('89)
- ❏ ❏ 2 - Death by Chrystal ('93)

BUTLER, Gwendoline
Insp. John Coffin
- ❏ ❏ 1 - Dead in a Row ('57)
- ❏ ❏ 2 - The Dull Dead ('58)
- ❏ ❏ 3 - The Murdering Kind ('58)
- ❏ ❏ 4 - Death Lives Next Door ('60)
- ❏ ❏ 5 - Make Me a Murderer ('61)
- ❏ ❏ 6 - Coffin in Oxford ('62)
- ❏ ❏ 7 - A Coffin for Baby ('63)
- ❏ ❏ 8 - Coffin Waiting ('64)
- ❏ ❏ 9 - A Nameless Coffin ('66)
- ❏ ❏ 10 - Coffin Following ('68)
- ❏ ❏ 11 - Coffin's Dark Number ('69)
- ❏ ❏ 12 - A Coffin from the Past ('70)
- ❏ ❏ 13 - A Coffin for the Canary ('74)
        [U.S.-Sarsen Place]
- ❏ ❏ 14 - Coffin on the Water ('86)
- ❏ ❏ 15 - Coffin in Fashion ('87)
- ❏ ❏ 16 - Coffin Underground ('88)
- ❏ ❏ 17 - Coffin in the Black Museum ('89)
- ❏ ❏ 18 - Coffin in the Museum of Crime ('89)
- ❏ ❏ 19 - Coffin and the Paper Man ('91)
- ❏ ❏ 20 - Coffin on Murder Street ('92)
- ❏ ❏ 21 - Cracking Open a Coffin ('93)
- ❏ ❏ 22 - A Coffin for Charley ('94)
- ❏ ❏ 23 - The Coffin Tree ('94)

C

CAIL, Carol
Maxey Burnell
❑ ❑ 1 - Private Lies ('93)
❑ ❑ 2 - Unsafe Keeping ('95)

CANNELL, Dorothy
Ellie & Ben Haskell with the Tramwell sisters
❑ ❑ 1 - The Thin Woman ('84)
❑ ❑ 2 - Down the Garden Path: A Pastoral Mystery ('85)
❑ ❑ 3 - The Widow's Club ('88) ☆ ☆
❑ ❑ 4 - Mum's the Word ('90)
❑ ❑ 5 - Femmes Fatal ('92)
❑ ❑ 6 - How to Murder Your Mother-in-law ('94)
❑ ❑ 7 - How to Murder the Man of Your Dreams ('95)

CANNON, Taffy
Nan Robinson
❑ ❑ 1 - A Pocketful of Karma ('93)
❑ ❑ 2 - Tangled Roots ('95)

CARLSON, P. M.
Maggie Ryan
❑ ❑ 1 - Audition for Murder ('85)
❑ ❑ 2 - Murder Is Academic ('85) ☆
❑ ❑ 3 - Murder Is Pathological ('86)
❑ ❑ 4 - Murder Unrenovated ('87) ☆ ☆
❑ ❑ 5 - Rehearsal for Murder ('88)
❑ ❑ 6 - Murder in the Dog Days ('90) ☆
❑ ❑ 7 - Murder Misread ('90)
❑ ❑ 8 - Bad Blood ('91)
Martine LaForte Hopkins
❑ ❑ 1 - Gravestone ('92) ☆ ☆ ☆ ☆
❑ ❑ 2 - Bloodstream ('95)

CAUDWELL, Sarah 🄿
Hilary Tamar
❑ ❑ 1 - Thus Was Adonis Murdered ('81)
❑ ❑ 2 - The Shortest Way to Hades ('85)
❑ ❑ 3 - The Sirens Sang of Murder ('89) ★ ☆

? What is the most popular name for a woman detective, whether cop, P.I. or amateur?

CHALLIS, Mary ▣
Jeremy Locke
- ❏ ❏ 1 - Burden of Proof ('80)
- ❏ ❏ 2 - Crimes Past ('80)
- ❏ ❏ 3 - The Ghost of an Idea ('81)
- ❏ ❏ 4 - A Very Good Hater ('81)

CHAPMAN, Sally
Juliet Blake
- ❏ ❏ 1 - Raw Data ('91)
- ❏ ❏ 2 - Love Bytes ('94)
- ❏ ❏ 3 - Cyber Kiss ('96)

CHARLES, Kate ▣
Lucy Kingsley & David Middleton-Brown
- ❏ ❏ 1 - A Deadly Drink of Wine ('91)
- ❏ ❏ 2 - The Snares of Death ('93)
- ❏ ❏ 3 - Appointed to Die ('94)
- ❏ ❏ 4 - A Dead Man Out of Mind ('95)

CHASE, Elaine Raco
Nikki Holden & Roman Cantrell
- ❏ ❏ 1 - Dangerous Places ('87)
- ❏ ❏ 2 - Dark Corners ('88)

CHISHOLM, P. F. ▣
Sir Robert Carey
- ❏ ❏ 1 - A Famine of Horses ('95)
- ❏ ❏ 2 - A Season of Knives ('96)

CHRISTIE, Agatha
Hercule Poirot
- ❏ ❏ 1 - The Mysterious Affair at Styles ('20)
- ❏ ❏ 2 - Murder on the Links ('23)
- ❏ ❏ 3 - The Murder of Roger Ackroyd ('26)
- ❏ ❏ 4 - The Big Four ('27)
- ❏ ❏ 5 - The Mystery of the Blue Train ('28)
- ❏ ❏ 6 - Dead Man's Mirror ('31)
- ❏ ❏ 7 - Peril at End House ('31)
- ❏ ❏ 8 - Lord Edgeware Dies ('33)
  [U.S.-Thirteen at Dinner]
- ❏ ❏ 9 - Three-Act Tragedy ('34)
  [U.S.-Murder in Three Acts]
- ❏ ❏ 10 - Murder on the Orient Express ('34)
  [U.S.-Murder in the Calais Coach]

❑ ❑ 11 - Death in the Clouds ('35)
   [U.S.-Death in the Air]
❑ ❑ 12 - Murder in Mesopotamia ('36)
❑ ❑ 13 - Cards on the Table ('36)
❑ ❑ 14 - The ABC Murders ('36)
   [U.S.-The Alphabet Murders]
❑ ❑ 15 - Dumb Witness ('37)
   [U.S.-Poirot Loses a Client]
❑ ❑ 16 - Death on the Nile ('37)
❑ ❑ 17 - Murder in the Mews ('37)
   [U.S.-Dead Man's Mirror]
❑ ❑ 18 - A Holiday for Murder ('38)
❑ ❑ 19 - Appointment with Death ('38)
❑ ❑ 20 - Hercule Poirot's Christmas ('38)
   [U.S.-Murder for Christmas]
❑ ❑ 21 - Sad Cypress ('39)
❑ ❑ 22 - One, Two, Buckle My Shoe ('40)
   [U.S.-The Patriotic Murders]
❑ ❑ 23 - Evil Under the Sun ('41)
❑ ❑ 24 - Five Little Pigs ('41)
   [U.S.-Murder in Retrospect]
❑ ❑ 25 - The Hollow ('46)
   [U.S.-Murder After Hours]
❑ ❑ 26 - Taken at the Flood ('48)
   [U.S.-There Is a Tide]
❑ ❑ 27 - Mrs. McGinty's Dead ('52)
   [U.S.-Blood Will Tell]
❑ ❑ 28 - After the Funeral ('53)
   [U.S.-Funerals are Fatal]
❑ ❑ 29 - Hickory, Dickory, Dock ('55)
   [U.S.-Hickory, Dickory, Death]
❑ ❑ 30 - Dead Man's Folly ('56)
❑ ❑ 31 - Cat Among the Pigeons ('59)
❑ ❑ 32 - The Clocks ('63)
❑ ❑ 33 - Third Girl ('66)
❑ ❑ 34 - Hallowe'en Party ('69)
❑ ❑ 35 - Elephants Can Remember ('72)
❑ ❑ 36 - Curtain ('75)

Miss Jane Marple
❑ ❑ 1 - The Murder at the Vicarage ('30)
❑ ❑ 2 - The Moving Finger ('42)
❑ ❑ 3 - The Body in the Library ('42)
❑ ❑ 4 - A Murder Is Announced ('50)
❑ ❑ 5 - They Do It with Mirrors ('52)
   [U.S.-Murder with Mirrors]

❑ ❑ 6 - A Pocket Full of Rye ('53)
❑ ❑ 7 - 4:50 from Paddington ('57)
     [U.S.-What Mrs. McGillicuddy Saw]
❑ ❑ 8 - The Mirror Crack'd from Side to Side ('62)
     [U.S.-The Mirror Crack'd]
❑ ❑ 9 - A Caribbean Mystery ('64)
❑ ❑ 10 - At Bertram's Hotel ('65)
❑ ❑ 11 - Nemesis ('71)
❑ ❑ 12 - Sleeping Murder ('76)

Tuppence & Tommy Beresford
❑ ❑ 1 - The Secret Adversary ('22)
❑ ❑ 2 - Partners in Crime [short stories] ('29)
❑ ❑ 3 - N or M? ('41)
❑ ❑ 4 - By the Pricking of My Thumbs ('68)
❑ ❑ 5 - Postern of Fate ('73)

CHRISTMAS, Joyce
Betty Trenka
❑ ❑ 1 - This Business Is Murder ('93)
❑ ❑ 2 - Death at Face Value ('95)

Lady Margaret Priam
❑ ❑ 1 - Suddenly in Her Sorbet ('88)
❑ ❑ 2 - Simply to Die For ('89)
❑ ❑ 3 - A Fete Worse than Death ('90)
❑ ❑ 4 - A Stunning Way to Die ('91)
❑ ❑ 5 - Friend or Faux ('91)
❑ ❑ 6 - It's Her Funeral ('92)
❑ ❑ 7 - A Perfect Day for Dying ('94)

CHURCHILL, Jill ℙ
Jane Jeffry
❑ ❑ 1 - Grime & Punishment ('89) ★ ★ ☆
❑ ❑ 2 - A Farewell to Yarns ('91)
❑ ❑ 3 - A Quiche Before Dying ('93)
❑ ❑ 4 - The Class Menagerie ('93)
❑ ❑ 5 - A Knife to Remember ('94)
❑ ❑ 6 - From Here to Paternity ('95)
❑ ❑ 7 - Silence of the Hams ('96)

CLARK, Carol Higgins
Regan Reilly
❑ ❑ 1 - Decked ('92) ☆
❑ ❑ 2 - Snagged ('93)
❑ ❑ 3 - Iced ('95)

CLARK, Carolyn Chambers
Megan Baldwin
- ❏ ❏ 1 - Deadlier Than Death ('93)

Theresa Franco
- ❏ ❏ 1 - Dangerous Alibis ('94)

CLARKE, Anna
Paula Glenning
- ❏ ❏ 1 - Last Judgment ('85)
- ❏ ❏ 2 - Cabin 3033 ('86)
- ❏ ❏ 3 - The Mystery Lady ('86)
- ❏ ❏ 4 - Murder in Writing ('88)
- ❏ ❏ 5 - The Whitelands Affair ('89)
- ❏ ❏ 6 - The Case of the Paranoid Patient ('91)
- ❏ ❏ 7 - The Case of the Ludicrous Letters ('94)

CLEARY, Melissa
Jackie Walsh & Jake
- ❏ ❏ 1 - A Tail of Two Murders ('92)
- ❏ ❏ 2 - Dog Collar Crime ('93)
- ❏ ❏ 3 - Hounded to Death ('93)
- ❏ ❏ 4 - Skull and Dog Bones ('94)
- ❏ ❏ 5 - First Pedigree Murder ('94)
- ❏ ❏ 6 - The Maltese Puppy ('95)

CLEEVES, Ann
George & Molly Palmer-Jones
- ❏ ❏ 1 - A Bird in the Hand ('86)
- ❏ ❏ 2 - Come Death and High Water ('87)
- ❏ ❏ 3 - Murder in Paradise ('89)
- ❏ ❏ 4 - A Prey to Murder ('89)
- ❏ ❏ 5 - Sea Fever ('91)
- ❏ ❏ 6 - Another Man's Poison ('93)
- ❏ ❏ 7 - The Mill on the Shore ('94)

Stephen Ramsey
- ❏ ❏ 1 - A Lesson in Dying ('90)
- ❏ ❏ 2 - Murder in My Backyard ('91)
- ❏ ❏ 3 - A Day in the Death of Dorothea Cassidy ('92)
- ❏ ❏ 4 - Killjoy ('95)

CODY, Liza 🅿
Anna Lee
- ❏ ❏ 1 - Dupe ('80) ★ ☆
- ❏ ❏ 2 - Bad Company ('82)
- ❏ ❏ 3 - Stalker ('84)

❑ ❑ 3 - A Bite of Death ('91)
❑ ❑ 4 - Paws Before Dying ('92)
❑ ❑ 5 - Gone to the Dogs ('92)
❑ ❑ 6 - Bloodlines ('92)
❑ ❑ 7 - Ruffly Speaking ('93)
❑ ❑ 8 - Black Ribbon ('95)

COOPER, Natasha 🄿

Willow King & Cressida Woodruffe
❑ ❑ 1 - Festering Lilies ('90)
         [U.S.–A Common Death]
❑ ❑ 2 - Poison Flowers ('91)
❑ ❑ 3 - Bloody Roses ('92)
❑ ❑ 4 - Bitter Herbs ('93)
❑ ❑ 5 - Rotten Apples ('95)

COOPER, Susan Rogers

E. J. Pugh
❑ ❑ 1 - One, Two, What Did Daddy Do? ('92)

Kimmey Kruse
❑ ❑ 1 - Funny as a Dead Comic ('93)
❑ ❑ 2 - Funny as a Dead Relative ('94)

Milton Kovak
❑ ❑ 1 - The Man in the Green Chevy ('88)
❑ ❑ 2 - Houston in the Rear View Mirror ('90)
❑ ❑ 3 - Other People's Houses ('90)
❑ ❑ 4 - Chasing Away the Devil ('91)
❑ ❑ 5 - Dead Moon on the Rise ('94)
❑ ❑ 6 - Doctors and Lawyers and Such ('95)

CORNWELL, Patricia

Kay Scarpetta
❑ ❑ 1 - Postmortem ('90) ★ ★ ★ ★
❑ ❑ 2 - Body of Evidence ('91)
❑ ❑ 3 - All That Remains ('92)
❑ ❑ 4 - Cruel and Unusual ('93) ★
❑ ❑ 5 - The Body Farm ('94)
❑ ❑ 6 - From Potter's Field ('95)

CRAIG, Alisa 🄿

Dittany Henbit Monk & Osbert Monk
❑ ❑ 1 - The Grub-and-Stakers Move a Mountain ('81)
❑ ❑ 2 - The Grub-and-Stakers Quilt a Bee ('85)
❑ ❑ 3 - The Grub-and-Stakers Pinch a Poke ('88)
❑ ❑ 4 - The Grub-and-Stakers Spin a Yarn ('90)
❑ ❑ 5 - The Grub-and-Stakers House a Haunt ('93)

Madoc & Janet Rhys
- ❑ ❑ 1 - A Pint of Murder ('80)
- ❑ ❑ 2 - Murder Goes Mumming ('81)
- ❑ ❑ 3 - A Dismal Thing to Do ('86)
- ❑ ❑ 4 - Trouble in the Brasses ('89)
- ❑ ❑ 5 - The Wrong Rite ('92)

CRANE, Frances
Pat & Jean Abbot
- ❑ ❑ 1 - The Turquoise Shop ('41)
- ❑ ❑ 2 - The Golden Box ('42)
- ❑ ❑ 3 - The Yellow Violet ('43)
- ❑ ❑ 4 - The Pink Umbrella ('43)
- ❑ ❑ 5 - The Applegreen Cat ('43)
- ❑ ❑ 6 - The Amethyst Spectacles ('44)
- ❑ ❑ 7 - The Indigo Necklace ('45)
- ❑ ❑ 8 - The Cinnamon Murder ('46)
- ❑ ❑ 9 - The Shocking Pink Hat ('46)
- ❑ ❑ 10 - Murder on the Purple Water ('47)
- ❑ ❑ 11 - Black Cypress ('48)
- ❑ ❑ 12 - The Flying Red Horse ('49)
- ❑ ❑ 13 - The Daffodil Blonde ('50)
- ❑ ❑ 14 - Murder in Blue Street ('51)
     [Britain-Murder in Blue Hour]
- ❑ ❑ 15 - The Polkadot Murder ('51)
- ❑ ❑ 16 - Thirteen White Tulips ('53)
- ❑ ❑ 17 - Murder in Bright Red ('53)
- ❑ ❑ 18 - The Coral Princess Murders ('54)
- ❑ ❑ 19 - Death in Lilac Time ('55)
- ❑ ❑ 20 - Horror on the Ruby X ('56)
- ❑ ❑ 21 - The Ultraviolet Widow ('56)
- ❑ ❑ 22 - The Man in Gray ('58)
     [Britain-The Gray Stranger]
- ❑ ❑ 23 - The Buttercup Case ('58)
- ❑ ❑ 24 - Death Wish Green ('60)
- ❑ ❑ 25 - The Amber Eyes ('62)
- ❑ ❑ 26 - The Body Beneath a Mandarin Tree ('65)

CRANE, Hamilton ℗
Emily D. Seeton
- ❑ ❑ 1 - Picture Miss Seeton ('68) ☆
- ❑ ❑ 2 - Miss Seeton Draws the Line ('69)
- ❑ ❑ 3 - Witch Miss Seeton ('71)
     [Britain-Miss Seeton, Bewitched]
- ❑ ❑ 4 - Miss Seeton Sings ('73)
- ❑ ❑ 5 - Odds on Miss Seeton ('75)

❑ ❑ 6 - Advantage Miss Seeton ('90)
❑ ❑ 7 - Miss Seeton at the Helm ('90)
❑ ❑ 8 - Miss Seeton, By Appointment ('90)
❑ ❑ 9 - Miss Seeton Cracks the Case ('91)
❑ ❑ 10 - Miss Seeton Paints the Town ('91)
❑ ❑ 11 - Miss Seeton Rocks the Cradle ('92)
❑ ❑ 12 - Hands Up, Miss Seeton ('92)
❑ ❑ 13 - Miss Seeton By Moonlight ('92)
❑ ❑ 14 - Miss Seeton Plants Suspicion ('93)
❑ ❑ 15 - Miss Seeton Goes to Bat ('93)
❑ ❑ 16 - Starring Miss Seeton ('94)
❑ ❑ 17 - Miss Seeton Undercover ('94)
❑ ❑ 18 - Miss Seeton Rules ('94)
❑ ❑ 19 - Sold to Miss Seeton ('95)

CRESPI, Camilla (Trella) 🅿

Simona Griffo

❑ ❑ 1 - The Trouble with a Small Raise ('91)
❑ ❑ 2 - The Trouble with Moonlighting ('91)
❑ ❑ 3 - The Trouble with Too Much Sun ('92)
❑ ❑ 4 - The Trouble with Thin Ice ('93)
❑ ❑ 5 - The Trouble with Going Home ('95)

CROMBIE, Deborah

Duncan Kincaid & Gemma James

❑ ❑ 1 - A Share in Death ('93) ☆
❑ ❑ 2 - All Shall Be Well ('94)
❑ ❑ 3 - Leave the Grave Green ('95)

CROSS, Amanda 🅿

Kate Fansler

❑ ❑ 1 - In the Last Analysis ('64) ☆
❑ ❑ 2 - The James Joyce Murder ('67)
❑ ❑ 3 - Poetic Justice ('70)
❑ ❑ 4 - The Theban Mysteries ('72)
❑ ❑ 5 - The Question of Max ('76)
❑ ❑ 6 - Death in a Tenured Position ('81)
❑ ❑ 7 - Sweet Death, Kind Death ('84)
❑ ❑ 8 - No Word from Winifred ('86)
❑ ❑ 9 - A Trap for Fools ('89)
❑ ❑ 10 - The Players Come Again ('90)
❑ 11 - An Imperfect Spy ('95)

What P.I. in ancient Rome is a reluctant informer for the emperor Vespasian?

CROWLEIGH, Ann 🅿

Miranda & Clare Clively
- ❑ ❑ 1 - Dead as Dead Can Be ('93)
- ❑ ❑ 2 - Wait for the Dark ('93)

CRUM, Laura

Gail McCarthy
- ❑ ❑ 1 - Cutter ('94)

CURZON, Clare 🅿

Mike Yeadings
- ❑ ❑ 1 - I Give You Five Days ('83)
- ❑ ❑ 2 - Masks and Faces ('84)
- ❑ ❑ 3 - The Trojan Hearse ('85)
- ❑ ❑ 4 - The Quest for K ('86)
- ❑ ❑ 5 - Three-Core Lead ('88)
- ❑ ❑ 6 - The Blue-Eyed Boy ('90)
- ❑ ❑ 7 - Cat's Cradle ('92)
- ❑ ❑ 8 - First Wife, Twice Removed ('93)
- ❑ ❑ 9 - Death Prone ('94)
- ❑ ❑ 10 - Nice People ('95)

--- 𝒟 ---

D'AMATO, Barbara

Cat Marsala
- ❑ ❑ 1 - Hardball ('90)
- ❑ ❑ 2 - Hard Tack ('91)
- ❑ ❑ 3 - Hard Luck ('92)
- ❑ ❑ 4 - Hard Women ('93)
- ❑ ❑ 5 - Hard Case ('94)
- ❑ ❑ 6 - Hard Christmas ('95)

Gerritt DeGraaf
- ❑ ❑ 1 - The Hands of Healing Murder ('80)
- ❑ ❑ 2 - The Eyes on Utopia Murders ('81)

Suze Figueroa & Norm Bennis
- ❑ ❑ 1 - KILLER.app ('96)

DAHEIM, Mary

Emma Lord
- ❑ ❑ 1 - The Alpine Advocate ('92) ☆
- ❑ ❑ 2 - The Alpine Betrayal ('93)
- ❑ ❑ 3 - The Alpine Christmas ('93)
- ❑ ❑ 4 - The Alpine Decoy ('94)
- ❑ ❑ 5 - The Alpine Escape ('95)

❑ ❑ 6 - The Alpine Fury ('95)
❑ ❑ 7 - The Alpine Gamble ('96)

Judith McMonigle
❑ ❑ 1 - Just Desserts ('91) ☆
❑ ❑ 2 - Fowl Prey ('91)
❑ ❑ 3 - Holy Terrors ('92)
❑ ❑ 4 - Dune to Death ('93)
❑ ❑ 5 - Bantam of the Opera ('93)
❑ ❑ 6 - Fit of Tempera ('94)
❑ ❑ 7 - Major Vices ('95)
❑ ❑ 8 - Murder My Suite ('95)
❑ ❑ 9 - Auntie Mayhem ('96)

DAIN, Catherine 🄿
Freddie O'Neal
❑ ❑ 1 - Lay It on the Line ('92) ☆
❑ ❑ 2 - Sing a Song of Death ('93)
❑ ❑ 3 - Walk a Crooked Mile ('94)
❑ ❑ 4 - Lament for a Dead Cowboy ('94) ☆
❑ ❑ 5 - Bet Against the House ('95)

DALY, Elizabeth
Henry Gamadge
❑ ❑ 1 - Unexpected Night ('40)
❑ ❑ 2 - Deadly Nightshade ('40)
❑ ❑ 3 - Murder in Volume 2 ('41)
❑ ❑ 4 - The House Without the Door ('42)
❑ ❑ 5 - Nothing Can Rescue Me ('43)
❑ ❑ 6 - Evidence of Things Seen ('43)
❑ ❑ 7 - Arrow Pointing Nowhere ('44)
❑ ❑ 8 - The Book of the Dead ('44)
❑ ❑ 9 - Any Shape or Form ('45)
❑ ❑ 10 - Somewhere in the House ('46)
❑ ❑ 11 - The Wrong Way Down ('46)
❑ ❑ 12 - Night Walk ('47)
❑ ❑ 13 - The Book of the Lion ('48)
❑ ❑ 14 - And Dangerous to Know ('49)
❑ ❑ 15 - Death and Letters ('50)
❑ ❑ 16 - The Book of the Crime ('51)
❑ ❑ 17 - Shroud for a Lady ('56)

DANK, Gloria
Bernard Woodrull & Arthur "Snooky" Randolph
❑ ❑ 1 - Friends Till the End ('89)
❑ ❑ 2 - Going Out in Style ('90)

DANKS, Denise
Georgina Powers
- ❑ ❑ 1 - User Deadly ('89)
  [Britain-The Pizza House Crash]
- ❑ ❑ 2 - Frame Grabber ('92)
- ❑ ❑ 3 - Wink a Hopeful Eye ('94)

DAVIDSON, Diane Mott
Goldy Bear
- ❑ ❑ 1 - Catering to Nobody ('90) ☆ ☆ ☆
- ❑ ❑ 2 - Dying for Chocolate ('92)
- ❑ ❑ 3 - Cereal Murders ('93)
- ❑ ❑ 4 - The Last Suppers ('94)
- ❑ ❑ 5 - Killer Pancake ('95)

DAVIS, Dorothy Salisbury
Jasper Tully & Mrs. Norris
- ❑ ❑ 1 - Death of an Old Sinner ('57)
- ❑ ❑ 2 - A Gentleman Called ('58)
- ❑ ❑ 3 - Old Sinners Never Die ('59)
Julie Hayes
- ❑ ❑ 1 - A Death in the Life ('76)
- ❑ ❑ 2 - Scarlet Night ('80)
- ❑ ❑ 3 - Lullaby of Murder ('84)
- ❑ ❑ 4 - The Habit of Fear ('87)

DAVIS, Lindsey
Marcus Didius Falco
- ❑ ❑ 1 - Silver Pigs ('89)
- ❑ ❑ 2 - Shadows in Bronze ('90)
- ❑ ❑ 3 - Venus in Copper ('91)
- ❑ ❑ 4 - Iron Hand of Mars ('92)
- ❑ ❑ 5 - Poseidon's Gold ('93)
- ❑ ❑ 6 - Last Act in Palmyra ('94)
- ❑ ❑ 7 - Time to Depart ('95)

DAWSON, Janet
Jeri Howard
- ❑ ❑ 1 - Kindred Crimes ('90) ★ ☆ ☆ ☆
- ❑ ❑ 2 - Till the Old Men Die ('93)
- ❑ ❑ 3 - Take a Number ('93)
- ❑ ❑ 4 - Don't Turn Your Back on the Ocean ('94)
- ❑ ❑ 5 - Nobody's Child ('95)

DAY, Dianne
Fremont Jones
- ❑ ❑ 1 - The Strange Files of Fremont Jones ('95)
- ❑ ❑ 2 - Fire and Fog and Fremont Jones ('96)
- ❑ ❑ 3 - The Bohemian Murders ('97)

DAY, Marele
Claudia Valentine
- ❑ ❑ 1 - The Life and Crimes of Harry Lavender ('88)
- ❑ ❑ 2 - The Case of the Chinese Boxes ('90)
- ❑ ❑ 3 - The Last Tango of Delores Delgado ('92) ★
- ❑ ❑ 4 - The Disappearance of Madalena Grimaldi ('94)

DE LA TORRE, Lillian
Dr. Samuel Johnson & James Boswell
- ❑ ❑ 1 - Dr. Sam: Johnson, Detector ('46)
- ❑ ❑ 2 - The Detections of Dr. Sam: Johnson ('60)
- ❑ ❑ 3 - The Return of Dr. Sam: Johnson, Detector ('84)
- ❑ ❑ 4 - The Exploits of Dr. Sam: Johnson ('87)

DENGLER, Sandy
Jack Prester
- ❑ ❑ 1 - Death Valley ('93)
- ❑ ❑ 2 - A Model Murder ('93)
- ❑ ❑ 3 - Murder on the Mount ('94)
- ❑ ❑ 4 - The Quick and the Dead ('95)
Sgt. Joe Rodriguez
- ❑ ❑ 1 - Cat Killer ('93)
- ❑ ❑ 2 - Mouse Trapped ('93)
- ❑ ❑ 3 - The Last Dinosaur ('94)
- ❑ ❑ 4 - Gila Monster ('94)

DENTINGER, Jane
Jocelyn O'Roarke
- ❑ ❑ 1 - Murder on Cue ('83)
- ❑ ❑ 2 - First Hit of the Season ('84)
- ❑ ❑ 3 - Death Mask ('88)
- ❑ ❑ 4 - Dead Pan ('92)
- ❑ ❑ 5 - The Queen Is Dead ('94)
- ❑ ❑ 6 - Who Dropped Peter Pan? ('95)

DERESKE, Jo
Helma Zukas
- ❑ ❑ 1 - Miss Zukas and the Library Murders ('94)
- ❑ ❑ 2 - Miss Zukas and the Island Murders ('95)
- ❑ ❑ 3 - Miss Zukas and the Stroke of Death ('96)

DIETZ, Denise
Ellie Bernstein
- ❏ ❏ 1 - Throw Darts at a Cheesecake ('93)
- ❏ ❏ 2 - Beat Up a Cookie ('94)

DISNEY, Doris Miles
Jeff Di Marco
- ❏ ❏ 1 - Dark Road ('46)
- ❏ ❏ 2 - Family Skeleton ('49)
- ❏ ❏ 3 - Straw Man ('51)
  [Britain-The Case of the Straw Man]
- ❏ ❏ 4 - Trick or Treat ('55)
  [Britain-The Halloween Murder]
- ❏ ❏ 5 - Method in Madness ('57)
  [Britain-Quiet Violence]
- ❏ ❏ 6 - Did She Fall or Was She Pushed? ('59)
- ❏ ❏ 7 - Find the Woman ('62)
- ❏ ❏ 8 - The Chandler Policy ('71)
Jim O'Neill
- ❏ ❏ 1 - Compound for Death ('43)
- ❏ ❏ 2 - Murder on a Tangent ('45)
- ❏ ❏ 3 - Appointment at Nine ('47)
- ❏ ❏ 4 - Fire at Will ('50)
- ❏ ❏ 5 - The Last Straw ('54)
  [Britain-Driven to Kill]

DOLSON, Hildegarde
Lucy Ramsdale & James McDougal
- ❏ ❏ 1 - To Spite Her Face ('71) ☆
- ❏ ❏ 2 - A Dying Fall ('73)
- ❏ ❏ 3 - Please Omit Funeral ('75)
- ❏ ❏ 4 - Beauty Sleep ('77)

DOMINIC, R. B. 🄿
Ben Safford
- ❏ ❏ 1 - Murder Sunny Side Up ('68)
- ❏ ❏ 2 - Murder in High Place ('70)
- ❏ ❏ 3 - There Is No Justice ('71)
- ❏ ❏ 4 - Epitaph for a Lobbyist ('74)
- ❏ ❏ 5 - Murder out of Commission ('76)
- ❏ ❏ 6 - The Attending Physician ('80)
- ❏ ❏ 7 - Unexpected Developments ('84)

DONALD, Anabel
Alex Tanner
- ❑ ❑ 1 - Smile, Honey ('91)
- ❑ ❑ 2 - An Uncommon Murder ('93)
- ❑ ❑ 3 - In at the Deep End ('94)
- ❑ ❑ 4 - The Glass Ceiling ('95)

DOUGLAS, Carole Nelson
Irene Adler
- ❑ ❑ 1 - Good Night, Mr. Holmes ('90) ★
- ❑ ❑ 2 - Good Morning, Irene ('90)
- ❑ ❑ 3 - Irene at Large ('92)
- ❑ ❑ 4 - Irene's Last Waltz ('94)
Dr. Kevin Blake
- ❑ ❑ 1 - Probe ('85)
- ❑ ❑ 2 - Counterprobe ('90)
Temple Barr & Midnight Louie
- ❑ ❑ 1 - Catnap ('92)
- ❑ ❑ 2 - Pussyfoot ('93)
- ❑ ❑ 3 - Cat on a Blue Monday ('94)
- ❑ ❑ 4 - Cat in a Crimson Haze ('95)

DOUGLAS, Lauren Wright
Caitlin Reece
- ❑ ❑ 1 - The Always Anonymous Beast ('87)
- ❑ ❑ 2 - Ninth Life ('89)
- ❑ ❑ 3 - The Daughters of Artemis ('91)
- ❑ ❑ 4 - A Tiger's Heart ('92)
- ❑ ❑ 5 - Goblin Market ('93)
- ❑ ❑ 6 - A Rage of Maidens ('94)

DRAKE, Alison 🄿
Aline Scott
- ❑ ❑ 1 - Tango Key ('88)
- ❑ ❑ 2 - Fevered ('88)
- ❑ ❑ 3 - Black Moon ('89)
- ❑ ❑ 4 - High Strangeness ('92)

DREHER, Sarah
Stoner McTavish
- ❑ ❑ 1 - Stoner McTavish ('85)
- ❑ ❑ 2 - Something Shady ('86)
- ❑ ❑ 3 - Gray Magic ('87)
- ❑ ❑ 4 - A Captive in Time ('90)
- ❑ ❑ 5 - Otherworld ('93)
- ❑ ❑ 6 - Bad Company ('95)

DUFFY, Margaret

Ingrid Langley & Patrick Gillard
- ❏ ❏ 1 - A Murder of Crows ('87)
- ❏ ❏ 2 - Death of a Raven ('88)
- ❏ ❏ 3 - Brass Eagle ('89)
- ❏ ❏ 4 - Who Killed Cock Robin? ('90)
- ❏ ❏ 5 - Rook-Shoot ('91)

Joanna McKenzie
- ❏ ❏ 1 - Dressed to Kill ('94)

DUNANT, Sarah

Hannah Wolfe
- ❏ ❏ 1 - Birth Marks ('92)
- ❏ ❏ 2 - Fat Lands ('93) ★
- ❏ ❏ 3 - Under My Skin ('95)

Marla Masterson
- ❏ ❏ 1 - Snowstorms in a Hot Climate ('88)

DUNBAR, Sophie

Claire & Dan Claiborne
- ❏ ❏ 1 - Behind Eclaire's Doors ('93)
- ❏ ❏ 2 - Redneck Riviera ('95)
- ❏ ❏ 3 - A Bad Hair Day ('96)

DUNLAP, Susan

Jill Smith
- ❏ ❏ 1 - Karma ('81)
- ❏ ❏ 2 - As a Favor ('84)
- ❏ ❏ 3 - Not Exactly a Brahmin ('85)
- ❏ ❏ 4 - Too Close to the Edge ('87)
- ❏ ❏ 5 - A Dinner to Die For ('87)
- ❏ ❏ 6 - Diamond in the Buff ('90)
- ❏ ❏ 7 - Death and Taxes ('92)
- ❏ ❏ 8 - Time Expired ('93)
- ❏ ❏ 9 - Sudden Exposure ('96)

Kiernan O'Shaughnessy
- ❏ ❏ 1 - Pious Deception ('89)
- ❏ ❏ 2 - Rogue Wave ('91)
- ❏ ❏ 3 - High Fall ('94)

Vejay Haskell
- ❏ ❏ 1 - An Equal Opportunity Death ('83)
- ❏ ❏ 2 - The Bohemian Connection ('85)
- ❏ ❏ 3 - The Last Annual Slugfest ('86)

DUNN, Carola
Daisy Dalrymple
- ❏ ❏ 1 - Death at Wentwater Court ('94)
- ❏ ❏ 2 - The Winter Garden Mystery ('95)

DUNNETT, Dorothy ▣
Johnson Johnson
- ❏ ❏ 1 - The Photogenic Soprano ('68)
  [Britain-Dolly and the Singing Bird]
- ❏ ❏ 2 - Murder in the Round ('70)
  [Britain-Dolly and the Cookie Bird]
- ❏ ❏ 3 - Match for a Murderer ('71)
  [Britain-Dolly and the Doctor Bird]
- ❏ ❏ 4 - Murder in Focus ('72)
  [Britain-Dolly and the Starry Bird]
- ❏ ❏ 5 - Split Code ('76)
  [Britain-Dolly and the Nanny Bird]
- ❏ ❏ 6 - Tropical Issue ('83)
  [Britain-Dolly and the Bird of Paradise]
- ❏ ❏ 7 - Moroccan Traffic ('92)
  [Britain-Send a Fax to the Kasbah]

DYMMOCH, Michael Allen ▣
John Thinnes & Dr. Jack Caleb
- ❏ ❏ 1 - The Man Who Understood Cats ('93) ★
- ❏ ❏ 2 - The Death of Blue Mountain Cat ('95)

ℰ

EBERHART, Mignon G.
Sarah Keate & Lance O'Leary
- ❏ ❏ 1 - The Patient in Room 18 ('29)
- ❏ ❏ 2 - While the Patient Slept ('30)
- ❏ ❏ 3 - The Mystery of Hunting's End ('30)
- ❏ ❏ 4 - From This Dark Stairway ('31)
- ❏ ❏ 5 - Murder by an Aristocrat ('32)
- ❏ ❏ 6 - Wolf in Man's Clothing ('42)
- ❏ ❏ 7 - Man Missing ('54)

What newspaper correspondent turned mystery writer was elected the first woman president of the Mystery Writers of America? She was once the London art critic for the New York Times.

ECCLES, Marjorie
Gil Mayo
- ❏ ❏ 1 - Cast a Cold Eye ('88)
- ❏ ❏ 2 - Death of a Good Woman ('89)
- ❏ ❏ 3 - Requiem for a Dove ('90)
- ❏ ❏ 4 - More Deaths Than One ('90)
- ❏ ❏ 5 - Late of This Parish ('92)

EDGHILL, Rosemary 🅿
Karen Hightower
- ❏ ❏ 1 - Speak Daggers to Her ('94)
- ❏ ❏ 2 - Book of Moons ('95)

EDWARDS, Ruth Dudley
James Milton & Robert Amiss
- ❏ ❏ 1 - Corridors of Death ('81)
- ❏ ❏ 2 - St. Valentine's Day Murders ('85)
- ❏ ❏ 3 - The English School of Murder ('90)
       [APA-The School of English Murder]
- ❏ ❏ 4 - Clubbed to Death ('92)
- ❏ ❏ 5 - Matricide at St. Martha's ('94)

EGAN, Lesley 🅿
Jesse Falkenstein
- ❏ ❏ 1 - A Case for Appeal [includes Vic Varallo] ('61)
- ❏ ❏ 2 - Against the Evidence ('62)
- ❏ ❏ 3 - My Name Is Death ('64)
- ❏ ❏ 4 - Some Avenger, Rise ('66)
- ❏ ❏ 5 - A Serious Investigation ('68)
- ❏ ❏ 6 - In the Death of a Man ('70)
- ❏ ❏ 7 - Paper Chase ('72)
- ❏ ❏ 8 - The Blind Search ('77)
- ❏ ❏ 9 - Back on Death ('78)
- ❏ ❏ 10 - Motive in Shadow ('80)
- ❏ ❏ 11 - The Miser ('81)
- ❏ ❏ 12 - Little Boy Lost ('83)
- ❏ ❏ 13 - The Wine of Life ('85)
Vic Varallo
- ❏ ❏ 1 - The Borrowed Alibi ('62)
- ❏ ❏ 2 - Run to Evil ('63)
- ❏ ❏ 3 - Detective's Due ('65)
- ❏ ❏ 4 - The Nameless Ones ('67)
- ❏ ❏ 5 - The Wine of Violence ('69)
- ❏ ❏ 6 - Malicious Mischief ('71)
- ❏ ❏ 7 - Scenes of Crime ('76)

EICHLER, Selma
Desiree Shapiro

ELKINS, Charlotte & Aaron
Lee Ofsted & Graham Sheldon

ELROD, P. N.
Jack Fleming

ENNIS, Catherine
Dr. Bernadette Hebert

ERSKINE, Margaret ₧
Septimus Finch

❏ ❏ 7 - Dead by Now ('53)
❏ ❏ 8 - Fatal Relations ('55)
      [U.S.-Old Mrs. Ommanney Is Dead]
      [APA-The Dead Don't Speak]
❏ ❏ 9 - Sleep No More ('58)
❏ ❏ 10 - The House of the Enchantress ('59)
      [U.S.-A Graveyard Plot]
❏ ❏ 11 - The Woman at Belguardo ('61)
❏ ❏ 12 - The Case in Belmont Square ('63)
      [U.S.-No. 9 Belmont Square]
❏ ❏ 13 - Take a Dark Journey ('65)
      [U.S.-The Family at Tammerron]
❏ ❏ 14 - The Voice of Murder ('65)
❏ ❏ 15 - Case with Three Husbands ('67)
❏ ❏ 16 - The Ewe Lamb ('68)
❏ ❏ 17 - The Case of Mary Fielding ('70)
❏ ❏ 18 - The Brood of Folly ('71)
❏ ❏ 19 - Besides the Wench Is Dead ('73)
❏ ❏ 20 - Harriet Farewell ('75)
❏ ❏ 21 - The House in Hook Street ('78)

EVANOVICH, Janet
Stephanie Plum
❏ ❏ 1 - One for the Money ('94) ☆ ☆ ☆ ☆
❏ ❏ 2 - Two for the Dough ('96)

EYRE, Elizabeth 🄿
Sigismondo
❏ ❏ 1 - Death of the Duchess ('92)
❏ ❏ 2 - Curtains for the Cardinal ('93)
❏ ❏ 3 - Poison for the Prince ('94)
❏ ❏ 4 - Bravo for the Bride ('94)

F

FALLON, Ann C.
James Fleming
❏ ❏ 1 - Blood Is Thicker ('90)
❏ ❏ 2 - Where Death Lies ('91)
❏ ❏ 3 - Dead Ends ('92)
❏ ❏ 4 - Potter's Field ('93)
❏ ❏ 5 - Hour of Our Death ('95)

FARRELL, Gillian B.
Annie McGrogan
- ❑ ❑ 1 - Alibi for an Actress ('92)
- ❑ ❑ 2 - Murder and a Muse ('94)

FAWCETT, Quinn 🅟
Victoire Vernet
- ❑ ❑ 1 - Napoleon Must Die ('93)
- ❑ ❑ 2 - Death Wears a Crown ('93)

FEDDERSEN, Connie
Amanda Hazard
- ❑ ❑ 1 - Dead in the Water ('93)
- ❑ ❑ 2 - Dead in the Cellar ('94)
- ❑ ❑ 3 - Dead in the Melon Patch ('95)

FEMLING, Jean
Martha "Moz" Brant
- ❑ ❑ 1 - Hush, Money ('89)
- ❑ ❑ 2 - Getting Mine ('91)

FENISONG, Ruth
Gridley Nelson
- ❑ ❑ 1 - Murder Needs a Face ('42)
- ❑ ❑ 2 - Murder Needs a Name ('42)
- ❑ ❑ 3 - The Butler Died in Brooklyn ('43)
- ❑ ❑ 4 - Murder Runs a Fever ('43)
- ❑ ❑ 5 - Grim Rehearsal ('50)
- ❑ ❑ 6 - Dead Yesterday ('51)
- ❑ ❑ 7 - Deadlock ('52)
- ❑ ❑ 8 - The Wench Is Dead ('53)
- ❑ ❑ 9 - Miscast for Murder ('54)
  [APA-Too Lovely to Live]
- ❑ ❑ 10 - Bite the Hand ('56)
  [Britain-The Blackmailer]
- ❑ ❑ 11 - Death of the Party ('58)
- ❑ ❑ 12 - But Not Forgotten ('60)
  [Britain-Sinister Assignment]
- ❑ ❑ 13 - Dead Weight ('62)

FENNELLY, Tony
Margo Fortier
- ❑ ❑ 1 - The Hippie in the Wall ('94)
- ❑ ❑ 2 - 1(900)D-E-A-D ('96)

Matthew Arthur Sinclair
- ❏ ❏ 1 - The Glory Hole Murders ('85) ☆
- ❏ ❏ 2 - The Closet Hanging ('87)
- ❏ ❏ 3 - Kiss Yourself Goodbye ('89)

FERRARS, E. X. ▣

Andrew Basnett
- ❏ ❏ 1 - Something Wicked ('83)
- ❏ ❏ 2 - Root of All Evil ('84)
- ❏ ❏ 3 - The Crime and the Crystal ('85)
- ❏ ❏ 4 - The Other Devil's Name ('86)
- ❏ ❏ 5 - A Murder Too Many ('88)
- ❏ ❏ 6 - Smoke Without Fire ('90)
- ❏ ❏ 7 - A Hobby of Murder ('94)

Supt. Ditteridge
- ❏ ❏ 1 - A Stranger and Afraid ('71)
- ❏ ❏ 2 - Foot in the Grave ('73)

Toby Dyke
- ❏ ❏ 1 - Give a Corpse a Bad Name ('40)
  [U.S.-Rehearsals for Murder]
- ❏ ❏ 2 - Remove the Bodies ('40)
  [U.S.-Rehearsals for Murder]
- ❏ ❏ 3 - Death in Botanist's Bay ('41)
  [U.S.-Murder of a Suicide]
- ❏ ❏ 4 - Don't Monkey with Murder ('42)
  [U.S.-The Shape of a Stain]
- ❏ ❏ 5 - Your Neck in a Noose ('42)
  [U.S.-Neck in a Noose]

Virginia & Felix Freer
- ❏ ❏ 1 - Last Will and Testament ('78)
- ❏ ❏ 2 - In at the Kill ('78)
- ❏ ❏ 3 - Frog in the Throat ('80)
- ❏ ❏ 4 - Thinner than Water ('81)
- ❏ ❏ 5 - Death of a Minor Character ('83)
- ❏ ❏ 6 - I Met Murder ('85)
- ❏ ❏ 7 - Woman Slaughter ('89)
- ❏ ❏ 8 - Sleep of the Unjust ('90)
- ❏ ❏ 9 - Beware of the Dog ('92)

FICKLING, G. G. ▣

Erik March
- ❏ ❏ 1 - The Case of the Radioactive Redhead ('63)
- ❏ ❏ 2 - The Crazy Mixed-Up Nude ('64)
- ❏ ❏ 3 - Stiff as a Broad ('72)

Honey West
- ❑ ❑ 1 - This Girl for Hire ('57)
- ❑ ❑ 2 - Girl on the Loose ('58)
- ❑ ❑ 3 - A Gun for Honey ('58)
- ❑ ❑ 4 - Girl on the Prowl ('59)
- ❑ ❑ 5 - Honey in the Flesh ('59)
- ❑ ❑ 6 - Dig a Dead Doll ('60)
- ❑ ❑ 7 - Kiss for a Killer ('60)
- ❑ ❑ 8 - Blood and Honey ('61)
- ❑ ❑ 9 - Bombshell ('64)
- ❑ ❑ 10 - Honey on Her Tail ('71)
- ❑ ❑ 11 - Stiff as a Broad ('72)

FLORA, Kate Clark
Ross McIntyre
- ❑ ❑ 1 - Silent Buddy ('95)

Thea Kozak
- ❑ ❑ 1 - Chosen for Death ('94)
- ❑ ❑ 2 - Death in a Funhouse Mirror ('95)

FLORIAN, S. L.
Viscountess Delia Ross-Merlani
- ❑ ❑ 1 - Born to the Purple ('92)

FOLEY, Rae 🅿
Hiram Potter
- ❑ ❑ 1 - Death and Mr. Potter ('55)
  [APA-The Peacock Is a Bird of Prey]
- ❑ ❑ 2 - The Last Gamble ('56)
- ❑ ❑ 3 - Run for Your Life ('56)
- ❑ ❑ 4 - Where Is Mary Bostwick? ('58)
  [APA-Escape to Fear]
- ❑ ❑ 5 - Dangerous to Me ('59)
- ❑ ❑ 6 - It's Murder Mr. Potter ('61)
  [APA-Curtain Call]
- ❑ ❑ 7 - Repent at Leisure ('62)
  [Britain-The Deadly Noose]
- ❑ ❑ 8 - Back Door to Death ('63)
  [APA-Nightmare Honeymoon]
- ❑ ❑ 9 - Fatal Lady ('64)
- ❑ ❑ 10 - Call It Accident ('65)
- ❑ ❑ 11 - A Calculated Risk ('70)

FORD, Leslie 🅿

Col. John Primrose & Grace Latham

- ❏ ❏ 1 - The Strangled Witness ('34)
- ❏ ❏ 2 - Ill-Met by Moonlight ('37)
- ❏ ❏ 3 - The Simple Way of Poison ('37)
- ❏ ❏ 4 - Three Bright Pebbles ('38)
- ❏ ❏ 5 - Reno Rendezvous ('39)
  [Britain-Mr. Cromwell Is Dead]
- ❏ ❏ 6 - False to Any Man ('39)
  [Britain-Snow-White Murder]
- ❏ ❏ 7 - Old Lover's Ghost ('40)
- ❏ ❏ 8 - The Murder of a Fifth Columnist ('41)
  [Britain-A Capital Crime]
- ❏ ❏ 9 - Murder in the O.P.M. ('42)
  [Britain-The Priority Murder]
- ❏ ❏ 10 - Siren in the Night ('43)
- ❏ ❏ 11 - All for the Love of a Lady ('44)
  [Britain-Crack of Dawn]
- ❏ ❏ 12 - The Philadelphia Murder Story ('45)
- ❏ ❏ 13 - Honolulu Story ('46)
  [Britain-Honolulu Murder Story]
- ❏ ❏ 14 - The Woman in Black ('47)
- ❏ ❏ 15 - The Devil's Stronghold ('48)
- ❏ ❏ 16 - Washington Whispers Murder ('53)
  [Britain-The Lying Jade]

FORREST, Katherine V.

Kate Delafield

- ❏ ❏ 1 - Amateur City ('84)
- ❏ ❏ 2 - Murder at the Nightwood Bar ('86)
- ❏ ❏ 3 - The Beverly Malibu ('89) ★
- ❏ ❏ 4 - Murder by Tradition ('91)

FOWLER, Earlene

Albenia "Benni" Harper

- ❏ ❏ 1 - Fool's Puzzle ('94) ☆
- ❏ ❏ 2 - Irish Chain ('95)
- ❏ ❏ 3 - Kansas Troubles ('96)

FRANKEL, Valerie

Wanda Mallory

- ❏ ❏ 1 - A Deadline for Murder ('91)
- ❏ ❏ 2 - Murder on Wheels ('92)
- ❏ ❏ 3 - Prime Time for Murder ('94)
- ❏ ❏ 4 - A Body to Die For ('95)

FRASER, Anthea
David Webb
- ❑ ❑ 1 - A Necessary End ('86)
- ❑ ❑ 2 - A Shroud for Delilah ('86)
- ❑ ❑ 3 - The Nine Bright Shiners ('88)
- ❑ ❑ 4 - Six Proud Walkers ('89)
- ❑ ❑ 5 - The Lily-White Boys ('91)
- ❑ ❑ 6 - Three, Three the Rivals ('92)
- ❑ ❑ 7 - The Gospel Makers ('94)

FRASER, Antonia
Jemima Shore
- ❑ ❑ 1 - Quiet as a Nun ('77)
- ❑ ❑ 2 - The Wild Island ('78)
- ❑ ❑ 3 - A Splash of Red ('81)
- ❑ ❑ 4 - Cool Repentance ('82)
- ❑ ❑ 5 - Oxford Blood ('85)
- ❑ ❑ 6 - Jemima Shore's First Case & Other Stories ('86)
- ❑ ❑ 7 - Your Royal Hostage ('87)
- ❑ ❑ 8 - The Cavalier Case ('91)
- ❑ ❑ 9 - Jemima Shore at the Sunny Grave
       [9 stories] ('93)
- ❑ ❑ 10 - Political Death ('94)

FRAZER, Margaret ▣
Sister Frevisse
- ❑ ❑ 1 - The Novice's Tale ('92)
- ❑ ❑ 2 - The Servant's Tale ('93) ☆
- ❑ ❑ 3 - The Outlaw's Tale ('94)
- ❑ ❑ 4 - The Bishop's Tale ('94)
- ❑ ❑ 5 - The Boy's Tale ('95)
- ❑ ❑ 6 - The Murderer's Tale ('96)

FRIEDMAN, Mickey ▣
Georgia Lee Maxwell
- ❑ ❑ 1 - Magic Mirror ('88)
       [Britain-Deadly Reflections]
- ❑ ❑ 2 - A Temporary Ghost ('89)

FROETSCHEL, Susan
Jane McBride
- ❑ ❑ 1 - Alaska Gray ('94)

FROME, David 🄿

Evan Pinkerton
- ❏ ❏ 1 - The Hammersmith Murders ('30)
- ❏ ❏ 2 - Two Against Scotland Yard ('31)
   [Britain-The By-Pass Murder]
- ❏ ❏ 3 - The Man from Scotland Yard ('32)
   [Britain–Mr. Simpson Finds a Body]
- ❏ ❏ 4 - The Eel Pie Murders ('33)
   [Britain-The Eel Pie Mystery]
- ❏ ❏ 5 - Mr. Pinkerton Goes to Scotland Yard ('34)
   [Britain-Arsenic in Richmond]
- ❏ ❏ 6 - Mr. Pinkerton Finds a Body ('34)
   [Britain-The Body in the Turl]
- ❏ ❏ 7 - Mr. Pinkerton Grows a Beard ('35)
   [Britain-The Body in Bedford Square]
- ❏ ❏ 8 - Mr. Pinkerton Has the Clue ('36)
- ❏ ❏ 9 - The Black Envelope ('37)
   [Britain-The Guilt Is Plain]
- ❏ ❏ 10 - Mr. Pinkerton at the Old Angel ('39)
   [Britain-Mr. Pinkerton and the Old Angel]
- ❏ ❏ 11 - Homicide House ('50)
   [Britain-Murder on the Square]

FROMER, Margot J.

Amanda Knight
- ❏ ❏ 1 - Scalpel's Edge ('91)
- ❏ ❏ 2 - Night Shift ('93)

FROMMER, Sara Hoskinson

Joan Spencer
- ❏ ❏ 1 - Murder in C Major ('93)
- ❏ ❏ 2 - Buried in Quilts ('94)

FULTON, Eileen

Nina McFall & Lt. Dino Rossi
- ❏ ❏ 1 - Take One for Murder ('88)
- ❏ ❏ 2 - Death of a Golden Girl ('88)
- ❏ ❏ 3 - Dying for Stardom ('88)
- ❏ ❏ 4 - Lights, Camera, Death ('88)
- ❏ ❏ 5 - A Setting for Murder ('88)
- ❏ ❏ 6 - Fatal Flashback ('89)

FURIE, Ruthe

Fran Kirk
- ❏ ❏ 1 - If Looks Could Kill ('95)
- ❏ ❏ 2 - Natural Death ('96)

FYFIELD, Frances 🅿

Helen West
- ❑ ❑ 1 - A Question of Guilt ('88) ☆ ☆ ☆
- ❑ ❑ 2 - Not That Kind of Place ('90)
     [Britain-Trial by Fire]
- ❑ ❑ 3 - Deep Sleep ('91)
- ❑ ❑ 4 - Shadow Play ('93)
- ❑ ❑ 5 - A Clear Conscience ('94)

Sarah Fortune
- ❑ ❑ 1 - Shadows on the Mirror ('89)
- ❑ ❑ 2 - Perfectly Pure and Good ('94)

═══════════════ 𝒢 ═══════════════

GALLISON, Kate

Mother Lavinia Grey
- ❑ ❑ 1 - Bury the Bishop ('95)

Nick Magaracz
- ❑ ❑ 1 - Unbalanced Accounts ('86)
- ❑ ❑ 2 - The Death Tape ('87)

GARDINER, Dorothy

Moss Magill
- ❑ ❑ 1 - What Crime Is It? ('56)
     [Britain-The Case of the Hula Clock]
- ❑ ❑ 2 - The Seventh Mourner ('58)
- ❑ ❑ 3 - Lion in Wait ('63)
     [Britain-Lion? or Murderer?]

Mr. Watson
- ❑ ❑ 1 - The Transatlantic Ghost ('33)
- ❑ ❑ 2 - A Drink for Mr. Cherry ('34)
     [Britain-Mr. Watson Intervenes]

GEASON, Susan

Syd Fish
- ❑ ❑ 1 - Shaved Fish ('93)
- ❑ ❑ 2 - Dogfish ('93)
- ❑ ❑ 3 - Sharkbait ('93)

GEORGE, Elizabeth

Thomas Lynley & Barbara Havers
- ❑ ❑ 1 - A Great Deliverance ('88) ★ ★ ☆ ☆
- ❑ ❑ 2 - Payment in Blood ('89)
- ❑ ❑ 3 - Well-Schooled in Murder ('90)
- ❑ ❑ 4 - A Suitable Vengeance ('91)

❏ ❏ 5 - For the Sake of Elena ('92)
❏ ❏ 6 - Missing Joseph ('93)
❏ ❏ 7 - Playing for the Ashes ('94)

GILBERT, Anthony 🅿

Arthur G. Crook

❏ ❏ 1 - Murder By Experts ('36)
❏ ❏ 2 - The Man Who Wasn't There ('37)
❏ ❏ 3 - Murder Has No Tongue ('37)
❏ ❏ 4 - Treason in My Breast ('38)
❏ ❏ 5 - The Bell of Death ('39)
❏ ❏ 6 - The Clock in the Hatbox ('39)
❏ ❏ 7 - Dear Dead Woman ('40)
      [U.S.-Death Takes a Redhead]
❏ ❏ 8 - The Vanishing Corpse ('41)
      [U.S.-She Vanished in the Dawn]
❏ ❏ 9 - The Woman in Red ('41)
      [APA-The Mystery of the Woman in Red]
❏ ❏ 10 - Something Nasty in the Woodshed ('42)
      [U.S.-Mystery in the Woodshed]
❏ ❏ 11 - The Case of the Tea-Cosy's Aunt ('42)
      [U.S.-Death in the Blackout]
      12 - The Mouse Who Wouldn't Play Ball ('43)
❏ ❏ 13 - He Came by Night ('44)
      [U.S.-Death at the Door]
❏ ❏ 14 - The Scarlet Button ('44)
      [APA-Murder Is Cheap]
❏ ❏ 15 - Don't Open the Door! ('45)
      [U.S.-Death Lifts the Latch]
❏ ❏ 16 - Lift Up the Lid ('45)
      [U.S.-The Innocent Bottle]
❏ ❏ 17 - The Black Stage ('45)
      [APA-Murder Cheats the Bride]
❏ ❏ 18 - The Spinster's Secret ('46)
      [U.S.-By Hook or By Crook]
❏ ❏ 19 - Death in the Wrong Room ('47)
❏ ❏ 20 - Die in the Dark ('47)
      [U.S.-The Missing Widow]
❏ ❏ 21 - Death Knocks Three Times ('49)
❏ ❏ 22 - A Nice Cup of Tea ('50)
      [U.S.-The Wrong Body]
❏ ❏ 23 - Murder Comes Home ('50)
❏ ❏ 24 - Lady Killer ('51)
❏ ❏ 25 - And Death Came Too ('52)
❏ ❏ 26 - Miss Pinnegar Disappears ('52)
      [U.S.-A Case for Mr. Crook]

❑ ❑ 27 - Footsteps Behind Me ('53)
     [U.S.-Black Death] [APA-Dark Death]
❑ ❑ 28 - Snake in the Grass ('54)
     [U.S.-Death Won't Wait]
❑ ❑ 29 - Is She Dead Too? ('55)
     [U.S.-A Question of Murder]
❑ ❑ 30 - Riddle of a Lady ('56)
❑ ❑ 31 - Give Death a Name ('57)
❑ ❑ 32 - Death Against the Clock ('58)
❑ ❑ 33 - Death Takes a Wife ('59)
     [U.S.-Death Casts a Long Shadow]
❑ ❑ 34 - Third Crime Lucky ('59)
     [U.S.-Prelude to Murder]
❑ ❑ 35 - Out for the Kill ('60)
❑ ❑ 36 - She Shall Die ('61)
     [U.S.-After the Verdict]
❑ ❑ 37 - Uncertain Death ('61)
❑ ❑ 38 - No Dust in the Attic ('62)
❑ ❑ 39 - Ring for a Noose ('63)
❑ ❑ 40 - Knock, Knock, Who's There? ('64)
     [U.S.-The Voice]
❑ ❑ 41 - The Fingerprint ('64)
❑ ❑ 42 - Passenger to Nowhere ('65)
❑ ❑ 43 - The Looking Glass Murder ('66)
❑ ❑ 44 - The Visitor ('67)
❑ ❑ 45 - Night Encounter ('68)
     [U.S.-Murder Anonymous]
❑ ❑ 46 - Missing from Her Home ('69)
❑ ❑ 47 - Death Wears a Mask ('70)
     [U.S.-Mr. Crook Lifts the Mask]
❑ ❑ 48 - Tenant for the Tomb ('71)
❑ ❑ 49 - Murder's a Waiting Game ('72)
❑ ❑ 50 - A Nice Little Killing ('74)

Scott Egerton

❑ ❑ 1 - The Tragedy at Freyne ('27)
❑ ❑ 2 - The Murder of Mrs. Davenport ('28)
❑ ❑ 3 - Death at Four Corners ('29)
❑ ❑ 4 - The Mystery of the Open Window ('29)
❑ ❑ 5 - The Night of the Fog ('30)
❑ ❑ 6 - The Body on the Beam ('32)
❑ ❑ 7 - The Long Shadow ('32)
❑ ❑ 8 - An Old Lady Dies ('34)
❑ ❑ 9 - The Man Who Was Too Clever ('35)

GILL, B. M. 🄿
Tom Maybridge
- ❑ ❑ 1 - Victims ('80)
  [U.S.-Suspect]
- ❑ ❑ 2 - Seminar for Murder ('85)
- ❑ ❑ 3 - The Fifth Rapunzel ('90)

GILMAN, Dorothy
Emily Pollifax
- ❑ ❑ 1 - The Unexpected Mrs. Pollifax ('66)
- ❑ ❑ 2 - The Amazing Mrs. Pollifax ('70)
- ❑ ❑ 3 - The Elusive Mrs. Pollifax ('71)
- ❑ ❑ 4 - A Palm for Mrs. Pollifax ('73)
- ❑ ❑ 5 - Mrs. Pollifax on Safari ('76)
- ❑ ❑ 6 - Mrs. Pollifax on the China Station ('83)
- ❑ ❑ 7 - Mrs. Pollifax and the Hong Kong Buddha ('85)
- ❑ ❑ 8 - Mrs. Pollifax and the Golden Triangle ('88)
- ❑ ❑ 9 - Mrs. Pollifax and the Whirling Dervish ('90)
- ❑ ❑ 10 - Mrs. Pollifax and the Second Thief ('93)
- ❑ ❑ 11 - Mrs. Pollifax Pursued ('95)
- ❑ ❑ 12 - Mrs. Pollifax and the Lion Killer ('96)

GILPATRICK, Noreen
Kate McLean
- ❑ ❑ 1 - Final Design ('93)

GIRDNER, Jaqueline
Kate Jasper
- ❑ ❑ 1 - Adjusted to Death ('91)
- ❑ ❑ 2 - The Last Resort ('91)
- ❑ ❑ 3 - Murder Most Mellow ('92)
- ❑ ❑ 4 - Fat-Free and Fatal ('93)
- ❑ ❑ 5 - Tea-Totally Dead ('94)
- ❑ ❑ 6 - A Stiff Critique ('95)
- ❑ ❑ 7 - Most Likely to Die ('96)

GIROUX, E. X. 🄿
Robert Forsythe & Abigail Sanderson
- ❑ ❑ 1 - A Death for Adonis ('84)
- ❑ ❑ 2 - A Death for a Darling ('85)
- ❑ ❑ 3 - A Death for a Dancer ('86)
- ❑ ❑ 4 - A Death for a Doctor ('86)
- ❑ ❑ 5 - A Death for a Dilletante ('87)
- ❑ ❑ 6 - A Death for a Dietician ('88)
- ❑ ❑ 7 - A Death for a Dreamer ('89)

❑ ❑ 8 - A Death for a Double ('90)
❑ ❑ 9 - A Death for a Dancing Doll ('91)
❑ ❑ 10 - A Death for a Dodo ('93)

GLASS, Leslie
April Woo
❑ ❑ 1 - Burning Time ('93)
❑ ❑ 2 - Hanging Time ('95)

GLEN, Alison 🄿
Charlotte Sams
❑ ❑ 1 - Showcase ('92)
❑ ❑ 2 - Trunk Show ('95)

GORDON, Alison
Kate Henry
❑ ❑ 1 - The Dead Pull Hitter ('89)
❑ ❑ 2 - Safe at Home ('91)
❑ ❑ 3 - Night Game ('93)
❑ ❑ 4 - Striking Out ('95)

GOSLING, Paula
Blackwater Bay Mystery
❑ ❑ 1 - A Few Dying Words ('94)
Jack Stryker & Kate Trevorne
❑ ❑ 1 - Monkey Puzzle ('85) ★
❑ ❑ 2 - Backlash ('89)
❑ ❑ 3 - The Body in Blackwater Bay ('92)
Luke Abbott
❑ ❑ 1 - The Wychford Murders ('86)
❑ ❑ 2 - Death Penalties ('91)

GRAFTON, Sue
Kinsey Millhone
❑ ❑ 1 - "A" is for Alibi ('82) ★ ☆
❑ ❑ 2 - "B" is for Burglar ('85) ★ ★
❑ ❑ 3 - "C" is for Corpse ('86) ★ ☆
❑ ❑ 4 - "D" is for Deadbeat ('87)
❑ ❑ 5 - "E" is for Evidence ('88)
❑ ❑ 6 - "F" is for Fugitive ('89)
❑ ❑ 7 - "G" is for Gumshoe ('90) ★ ★
❑ ❑ 8 - "H" is for Homicide ('91)
❑ ❑ 9 - "I" is for Innocent ('92) ★
❑ ❑ 10 - "J" is for Judgment ('93)
❑ ❑ 11 - "K" is for Killer ('94) ★ ☆
❑ ❑ 12 - "L" is for Lawless ('95)

GRAHAM, Caroline
Tom Barnaby
- ❏ ❏ 1 - The Killings at Badger's Drift ('87) ★ ☆
- ❏ ❏ 2 - Death of a Hollow Man ('89)
- ❏ ❏ 3 - Death in Disguise ('93)
- ❏ ❏ 4 - Written in Blood ('95)

GRANGER, Ann
Insp. Alan Markby & Meredith Mitchell
- ❏ ❏ 1 - Say it with Poison ('91)
- ❏ ❏ 2 - A Season for Murder ('92)
- ❏ ❏ 3 - Cold in the Earth ('93)
- ❏ ❏ 4 - Murder Among Us ('93)
- ❏ ❏ 5 - Where Old Bones Lie ('93)
- ❏ ❏ 6 - Flowers for His Funeral ('94)
- ❏ ❏ 7 - A Fine Place for Death ('95)

GRANT, Linda 🄿
Catherine Sayler
- ❏ ❏ 1 - Random Access Murder ('88) ☆
- ❏ ❏ 2 - Blind Trust ('90)
- ❏ ❏ 3 - Love Nor Money ('91) ☆
- ❏ ❏ 4 - A Woman's Place ('94)
- ❏ ❏ 5 - Lethal Genes ('96)

GRANT-ADAMSON, Lesley
Jim Rush
- ❏ ❏ 1 - A Life of Adventure ('92)
- ❏ ❏ 2 - Dangerous Games ('94)
Laura Flynn
- ❏ ❏ 1 - Too Many Questions ('91)
- ❏ ❏ 2 - The Dangerous Edge ('94)
Rain Morgan
- ❏ ❏ 1 - Death on Widow's Walk ('85)
- ❏ ❏ 2 - The Face of Death ('85)
- ❏ ❏ 3 - Guilty Knowledge ('86)
- ❏ ❏ 4 - Wild Justice ('87)
- ❏ ❏ 5 - Threatening Eye ('88)
- ❏ ❏ 6 - Curse the Darkness ('90)

GRAY, Dulcie 🄿
Insp. Supt. Cardiff
- ❏ ❏ 1 - Epitaph for a Dead Actor ('60)
- ❏ ❏ 2 - Died in the Red ('68)

GRAY, Gallagher 🄿

Theodore S. Hubbert & Auntie Lil

- ❏ ❏ 1 - Partners in Crime ('91)
- ❏ ❏ 2 - A Cast of Killers ('92)
- ❏ ❏ 3 - Death of a Dream Maker ('95)

GREEN, Anna Katherine

Caleb Sweetwater

- ❏ ❏ 1 - Agatha Webb (1899)
- ❏ ❏ 2 - The Woman in the Alcove (1906)
- ❏ ❏ 3 - The House of the Whispering Pines (1910)

Ebenezer Gryce

- ❏ ❏ 1 - The Leavenworth Case (1878)
- ❏ ❏ 2 - A Strange Disappearance (1880)
- ❏ ❏ 3 - Hand and Ring (1883)
- ❏ ❏ 4 - Behind Closed Doors (1888)
- ❏ ❏ 5 - A Matter of Millions (1890)
- ❏ ❏ 6 - The Doctor, His Wife, and the Clock (1895)
- ❏ ❏ 7 - That Affair Next Door (1897)
  [includes Mrs. Amelia Butterworth]
- ❏ ❏ 8 - Lost Man's Lane (1898)
  [includes Mrs. Amelia Butterworth]
- ❏ ❏ 9 - The Circular Study (1900)
  [includes Mrs. Amelia Butterworth]
- ❏ ❏ 10 - One of My Sons (1901)
- ❏ ❏ 11 - Initials Only (1911)
  [includes Caleb Sweetwater]
- ❏ ❏ 12 - The Mystery of the Hasty Arrow (1911)
  [includes Caleb Sweetwater]

GREEN, Christine

Connor O'Neill & Fran Wilson

- ❏ ❏ 1 - Death in the Country ('94)
- ❏ ❏ 2 - Die in My Dreams ('95)
- ❏ ❏ 3 - Fatal Cut ('96)

Kate Kinsella

- ❏ ❏ 1 - Deadly Errand ('91)
- ❏ ❏ 2 - Deadly Admirer ('92)
- ❏ ❏ 3 - Deadly Practice ('94)

? Who is the only woman to receive a lifetime achievement award from the Private Eye Writers of America?

GREEN, Edith Pinero

Dearborn V. Pinch

- ❑ ❑ 1 - Rotten Apples ('77)
- ❑ ❑ 2 - Sneaks ('79)
- ❑ ❑ 3 - Perfect Fools ('82)

GREEN, Kate

Theresa Fortunato & Oliver Jardino

- ❑ ❑ 1 - Shattered Moon ('86) ☆
- ❑ ❑ 2 - Black Dreams ('93)

GREENWOOD, Diane M.

Rev. Theodora Braithwaite

- ❑ ❑ 1 - Clerical Errors ('91)
- ❑ ❑ 2 - Unholy Ghosts ('92)
- ❑ ❑ 3 - Idol Bones ('93)
- ❑ ❑ 4 - Holy Terrors ('94)
- ❑ ❑ 5 - Every Deadly Sin ('95)

GREENWOOD, Kerry

Phryne Fisher

- ❑ ❑ 1 - Cocaine Blues ('89)
  [U.S.-Death by Misadventure]
- ❑ ❑ 2 - Flying Too High ('90)
- ❑ ❑ 3 - Murder on the Ballarat Train ('91)
- ❑ ❑ 4 - Death at Victoria Dock ('92)
- ❑ ❑ 5 - The Green Mill Murder ('93)
- ❑ ❑ 6 - Blood and Circuses ('94)
- ❑ ❑ 7 - Ruddy Gore ('95)
- ❑ ❑ 8 - Urn Burial ('96)

GRETH, Roma

Hana Shaner

- ❑ ❑ 1 - Now You Don't ('88)
- ❑ ❑ 2 - Plain Murder ('89)

GRIMES, Martha

Insp. Richard Jury

- ❑ ❑ 1 - The Man with a Load of Mischief ('81)
- ❑ ❑ 2 - The Old Fox Deceived ('82)
- ❑ ❑ 3 - The Anodyne Necklace ('83)
- ❑ ❑ 4 - The Dirty Duck ('84)
- ❑ ❑ 5 - Jerusalem Inn ('84)
- ❑ ❑ 6 - Help the Poor Struggler ('85)
- ❑ ❑ 7 - The Deer Leap ('85)

❏ ❏　8 - I Am the Only Running Footman ('86)
❏ ❏　9 - The Five Bells and Bladebone ('87)
❏ ❏　10 - The Old Silent ('89)
❏ ❏　11 - The Old Contemptibles ('90)
❏ ❏　12 - The Horse You Came in On ('93)
❏ ❏　13 - Rainbow's End ('95)

GRINDLE, Lucretia
H. W. Ross
❏ ❏　1 - The Killing of Ellis Martin ('93)
❏ ❏　2 - So Little to Die For ('94)

GUNNING, Sally
Peter Bartholomew
❏ ❏　1 - Hot Water ('90)
❏ ❏　2 - Under Water ('92)
❏ ❏　3 - Ice Water ('93)
❏ ❏　4 - Troubled Water ('93)
❏ ❏　5 - Rough Water ('94)
❏ ❏　6 - Still Water ('96)

GUR, Batya
Michael Ohayon
❏ ❏　1 - Saturday Morning Murder ('88)
❏ ❏　2 - Literary Murder ('93)
❏ ❏　3 - Murder on the Kibbutz: A Communal Case ('94) ☆

ℋ

HADDAD, Carolyn A.
Becky Belski
❏ ❏　1 - Caught in the Shadows ('92)

HADDAM, Jane 🅿
Gregor Demarkian
❏ ❏　1 - Not a Creature Was Stirring ('90) ☆ ☆
❏ ❏　2 - Precious Blood ('91)
❏ ❏　3 - Act of Darkness ('91)
❏ ❏　4 - Quoth the Raven ('91)
❏ ❏　5 - A Great Day for the Deadly ('92)
❏ ❏　6 - Feast of Murder ('92)
❏ ❏　7 - A Stillness in Bethlehem ('92)
❏ ❏　8 - Murder Superior ('92)
❏ ❏　9 - Festival of Deaths ('93)
❏ ❏　10 - Bleeding Hearts ('94)

❑ ❑ 11 - Dear Old Dead ('94)
❑ ❑ 12 - Fountain of Death ('95)

HADDOCK, Lisa
Carmen Ramirez
❑ ❑ 1 - Edited Out ('94)
❑ ❑ 2 - Final Cut ('95)

HAGER, Jean
Mitch Bushyhead
❑ ❑ 1 - The Grandfather Medicine ('89)
❑ ❑ 2 - Night Walker ('90)
❑ ❑ 3 - Ghostland ('92)
❑ ❑ 4 - The Fire Carrier ('96)
Molly Bearpaw
❑ ❑ 1 - Ravenmocker ('92)
❑ ❑ 2 - The Redbird's Cry ('94)
❑ ❑ 3 - Seven Black Stones ('95)
Tess Darcy
❑ ❑ 1 - Blooming Murder ('94)
❑ ❑ 2 - Dead and Buried ('95)
❑ ❑ 3 - Death on the Drunkard's Path ('96)

HALL, Mary Bowen
Emma Chizzit
❑ ❑ 1 - Emma Chizzit and the Queen Anne Killer ('89)
❑ ❑ 2 - Emma Chizzit and the Sacramento Stalker ('90)
❑ ❑ 3 - Emma Chizzit and the Napa Nemesis ('92)
❑ ❑ 4 - Emma Chizzit and the Mother Lode Marauder ('93)

HALL, Patricia
Alex Sinclair & Kate Weston
❑ ❑ 1 - The Poison Pool ('93)
Laura Ackroyd & Michael Thackeray
❑ ❑ 1 - Death by Election ('94)
❑ ❑ 2 - Dying Fall ('95)

HAMBLY, Barbara
James Asher
❑ ❑ 1 - Those Who Hunt the Night ('88)
❑ ❑ 2 - Traveling with the Dead ('95)

Who wrote 48 books about the barrister known as the British Perry Mason?

HAMILTON, Laurell K.
Anita Blake
- ❑ ❑ 1 - Guilty Pleasures ('93)
- ❑ ❑ 2 - The Laughing Corpse ('94)
- ❑ ❑ 3 - Circus of the Damned ('95)

HARDWICK, Mollie
Doran Fairweather
- ❑ ❑ 1 - Malice Domestic ('86)
- ❑ ❑ 2 - Parson's Pleasure ('87)
- ❑ ❑ 3 - Uneaseful Death ('88)
- ❑ ❑ 4 - The Bandersnatch ('89)
- ❑ ❑ 5 - Perish in July ('89)
- ❑ ❑ 6 - The Dreaming Damozel ('90)

HARRIS, Charlaine
Aurora Teagarden
- ❑ ❑ 1 - Real Murders ('90) ☆
- ❑ ❑ 2 - A Bone to Pick ('92)
- ❑ ❑ 3 - Three Bedrooms, One Corpse ('94)
- ❑ ❑ 4 - The Julius House ('95)
- ❑ ❑ 5 - Dead Over Heels ('96)

HARRIS, Lee 🄿
Christine Bennett
- ❑ ❑ 1 - The Good Friday Murder ('92) ☆
- ❑ ❑ 2 - The Yom Kippur Murder ('92)
- ❑ ❑ 3 - The Christening Day Murder ('93)
- ❑ ❑ 4 - The St. Patrick's Day Murder ('94)
- ❑ ❑ 5 - The Christmas Night Murder ('94)
- ❑ ❑ 6 - The Thanksgiving Day Murder ('95)
- ❑ ❑ 7 - The Passover Murder ('96)

HARRISON, Jamie
Jules Clement
- ❑ ❑ 1 - The Edge of the Crazies ('95)

HARROD-EAGLES, Cynthia
Bill Slider
- ❑ ❑ 1 - Orchestrated Death ('91)
- ❑ ❑ 2 - Death Watch ('92)
- ❑ ❑ 3 - Death to Go ('93) [APA-Necrochip]
- ❑ ❑ 4 - Grave Music ('94) [Britain-Dead End]

HART, Carolyn G.
Annie Laurance & Max Darling
- ❑ ❑ 1 - Death on Demand ('87) ☆ ☆
- ❑ ❑ 2 - Design for Murder ('87)
- ❑ ❑ 3 - Something Wicked ('88) ★ ★
- ❑ ❑ 4 - Honeymoon with Murder ('88) ★
- ❑ ❑ 5 - A Little Class on Murder ('89) ★ ☆ ☆
- ❑ ❑ 6 - Deadly Valentine ('90) ☆ ☆
- ❑ ❑ 7 - The Christie Caper ('91) ☆ ☆ ☆
- ❑ ❑ 8 - Southern Ghost ('92) ☆ ☆
- ❑ ❑ 9 - The Mint Julep Murder ('95)

Henrietta O'Dwyer Collins
- ❑ ❑ 1 - Dead Man's Island ('93) ★
- ❑ ❑ 2 - Scandal in Fair Haven ('94) ☆
- ❑ ❑ 3 - Death in Lovers' Lane ('96)

HART, Ellen 🄿
Jane Lawless
- ❑ ❑ 1 - Hallowed Murder ('89)
- ❑ ❑ 2 - Vital Lies ('91)
- ❑ ❑ 3 - Stage Fright ('92)
- ❑ ❑ 4 - A Killing Cure ('93)
- ❑ ❑ 5 - A Small Sacrifice ('94)
- ❑ ❑ 6 - Faint Praise ('95)

Sophie Greenway
- ❑ ❑ 1 - This Little Piggy Went to Murder ('94)
- ❑ ❑ 2 - For Every Evil ('95)

HART, Jeanne
Carl & Freda Pedersen
- ❑ ❑ 1 - Fetish ('87) ☆
  [Britain-A Personal Possession]
- ❑ ❑ 2 - Some Die Young ('90)
- ❑ ❑ 3 - Threnody for Two ('91)
  [Britain-Lament for Two Ladies]

HARTZMARK, Gini
Katherine Prescott Milholland
- ❑ ❑ 1 - Principal Defense ('92) ☆
- ❑ ❑ 2 - Final Option ('94)
- ❑ ❑ 3 - Bitter Business ('95)

? How many women have been named Grand Master by the Mystery Writers of America?

HAYMON, S. T.
Insp. Benjamin Jurnet
- ❑ ❑ 1 - Death and the Pregnant Virgin ('80)
- ❑ ❑ 2 - Ritual Murder ('82) ★
- ❑ ❑ 3 - Stately Homicide ('84)
- ❑ ❑ 4 - Death of a God ('87)
- ❑ ❑ 5 - A Very Particular Murder ('89)
- ❑ ❑ 6 - Death of a Warrior Queen ('91)
- ❑ ❑ 7 - A Beautiful Death ('94)

HAYTER, Sparkle
Robin Hudson
- ❑ ❑ 1 - What's a Girl Gotta Do? ('94) ★
- ❑ ❑ 2 - Nice Girls Finish Last ('96)

HEBERDEN, M. V.
Desmond Shannon
- ❑ ❑ 1 - Death on the Door Mat ('39)
- ❑ ❑ 2 - Fugitive from Murder ('40)
- ❑ ❑ 3 - Subscription to Murder ('40)
- ❑ ❑ 4 - Aces, Eights and Murder ('40)
- ❑ ❑ 5 - The Lobster Pick Murder ('40)
- ❑ ❑ 6 - Murder Follows Desmond Shannon ('42)
- ❑ ❑ 7 - Murder Makes a Racket ('42)
- ❑ ❑ 8 - Murder Goes Astray ('43)
- ❑ ❑ 9 - Murder of a Stuffed Shirt ('44)
- ❑ ❑ 10 - Vicious Pattern ('45)
- ❑ ❑ 11 - Drinks on the Victim ('47)
- ❑ ❑ 12 - They Can't All Be Guilty ('47)
- ❑ ❑ 13 - The Case of the Eight Brothers ('47)
- ❑ ❑ 14 - Exit This Way ('50)
  [APA-You'll Fry Tomorrow]
- ❑ ❑ 15 - That's the Spirit ('50)
  [Britain-Ghosts Can't Kill]
- ❑ ❑ 16 - Tragic Target ('52)
- ❑ ❑ 17 - Murder Unlimited ('53)

Rick Vanner
- ❑ ❑ 1 - Murder Cancels All Debts ('46)
- ❑ ❑ 2 - Engaged to Murder ('49)
- ❑ ❑ 3 - The Sleeping Witness ('51)

HENDRICKSON, Louise
Amy Prescott
- ❑ ❑ 1 - With Deadly Intent ('93)
- ❑ ❑ 2 - Grave Secrets ('94)
- ❑ ❑ 3 - Lethal Legacy ('95)

HENRY, Sue

Jessie Arnold & Alex Jensen
- ❑ ❑ 1 - Murder on the Iditarod Trail ('91) ★ ★
- ❑ ❑ 2 - Termination Dust ('95)
- ❑ ❑ 3 - Sleeping Lady ('96)

HERNDON, Nancy

Elena Jarvis
- ❑ ❑ 1 - Acid Bath ('95)
- ❑ ❑ 2 - Widows' Watch ('95)

HESS, Joan

Arly Hanks
- ❑ ❑ 1 - Malice in Maggody ('87)
- ❑ ❑ 2 - Mischief in Maggody ('88) ☆
- ❑ ❑ 3 - Much Ado in Maggody ('89)
- ❑ ❑ 4 - Mortal Remains in Maggody ('91)
- ❑ ❑ 5 - Madness in Maggody ('91)
- ❑ ❑ 6 - Maggody in Manhattan ('92)
- ❑ ❑ 7 - O Little Town of Maggody ('93) ☆ ☆
- ❑ ❑ 8 - Martians in Maggody ('94)
- ❑ ❑ 9 - Miracles in Maggody ('95)

Claire Malloy
- ❑ ❑ 1 - Strangled Prose ('86) ☆
- ❑ ❑ 2 - The Murder at the Murder at the Mimosa Inn ('86)
- ❑ ❑ 3 - Dear Miss Demeanor ('87)
- ❑ ❑ 4 - A Really Cute Corpse ('88)
- ❑ ❑ 5 - A Diet to Die For ('89) ★
- ❑ ❑ 6 - Roll Over and Play Dead ('91)
- ❑ ❑ 7 - Death by the Light of the Moon ('92)
- ❑ ❑ 8 - Poisoned Pins ('93)
- ❑ ❑ 9 - Tickled to Death ('94)
- ❑ ❑ 10 - Busy Bodies ('95)

HEYER, Georgette

Supt. Hannasyde
- ❑ ❑ 1 - Death in the Stocks ('35)
  [U.S.-Merely Murder]
- ❑ ❑ 2 - Behold, Here's Poison ('36)
- ❑ ❑ 3 - They Found Him Dead ('37)
- ❑ ❑ 4 - A Blunt Instrument ('38)

Insp. Hemingway
- ❑ ❑ 1 - No Wind of Blame ('39)
- ❑ ❑ 2 - Envious Casca ('41)
- ❑ ❑ 3 - Duplicate Death ('51)
- ❑ ❑ 4 - Detection Unlimited ('53)

HIGHSMITH, Domini
Father Simeon & Elvira
- ❏ ❏ 1 - Keeper at the Shrine ('95)

HIGHSMITH, Patricia
Tom Ripley
- ❏ ❏ 1 - The Talented Mr. Ripley ('55) ☆
- ❏ ❏ 2 - Ripley Underground ('70)
- ❏ ❏ 3 - Ripley's Game ('74)
- ❏ ❏ 4 - The Boy Who Followed Ripley ('80)
- ❏ ❏ 5 - Ripley Under Water ('92)

HIGHTOWER, Lynn S.
David Silver & String
- ❏ ❏ 1 - Alien Blues ('92)
- ❏ ❏ 2 - Alien Eyes ('93)
- ❏ ❏ 3 - Alien Heat ('94)
- ❏ ❏ 4 - Alien Rites ('95)

Lena Padget
- ❏ ❏ 1 - Satan's Lambs ('93) ★

Sonora Blair
- ❏ ❏ 1 - Flashpoint ('95)

HITCHENS, Dolores
Jim Sader
- ❏ ❏ 1 - Sleep with Strangers ('57)
- ❏ ❏ 2 - Sleep with Slander ('60)

HOLBROOK, Teri
Gale Grayson
- ❏ ❏ 1 - A Far and Deadly Cry ('95)
- ❏ ❏ 2 - The Grass Widow ('96)

HOLLAND, Isabelle
Rev. Claire Aldington
- ❏ ❏ 1 - The Lost Madonna ('83)
- ❏ ❏ 2 - A Death at St. Anselm's ('84)
- ❏ ❏ 3 - Flight of the Archangel ('85)
- ❏ ❏ 4 - A Lover Scorned ('86)
- ❏ ❏ 5 - A Fatal Advent ('89)
- ❏ ❏ 6 - The Long Search ('90)

HOLLINGSWORTH, Gerelyn
Frances Finn
- ❏ ❏ 1 - Murder at St. Adelaide's ('95)

HOLT, Hazel
Sheila Malory
- ❑ ❑ 1 - Mrs. Malory Investigates ('89)
  [Britain-Gone Away]
- ❑ ❑ 2 - The Cruellest Month ('91)
- ❑ ❑ 3 - Mrs. Malory and the Festival Murders ('93)
  [Britain-Uncertain Death]
- ❑ ❑ 4 - The Shortest Journey ('94)
- ❑ ❑ 5 - Mrs. Malory: Detective in Residence ('94)
  [Britain-Murder on Campus]
- ❑ ❑ 6 - Mrs. Malory Wonders Why ('95)
  [Britain-Superfluous Death]

HOLTZER, Susan
Anneke Haagen
- ❑ ❑ 1 - Something to Kill For ('94) ★
- ❑ ❑ 2 - Curly Smoke ('95)

HOOPER, Kay
Hagen
- ❑ ❑ 1 - Zach's Law ('87)
- ❑ ❑ 2 - Rafferty's Wife ('87)
- ❑ ❑ 3 - Raven on the Wing ('87)
- ❑ ❑ 4 - In Serena's Web ('87)
- ❑ ❑ 5 - Captain's Paradise ('88)
- ❑ ❑ 6 - Outlaw Derek ('88)
- ❑ ❑ 7 - Shades of Gray ('88)
- ❑ ❑ 8 - The Fall of Lucas Kendrick ('88)
- ❑ ❑ 9 - Unmasking Kelsey ('88)
- ❑ ❑ 10 - Aces High ('89)
- ❑ ❑ 11 - It Takes a Thief ('89)
Lane Montana & Trey Fortier
- ❑ ❑ 1 - Crime of Passion ('91)
- ❑ ❑ 2 - House of Cards ('91) ☆

HORANSKY, Ruby 🅿
Nikki Trakos
- ❑ ❑ 1 - Dead Ahead ('90)
- ❑ ❑ 2 - Dead Center ('94)

HORNSBY, Wendy
Kate Teague & Roger Tejeda
- ❑ ❑ 1 - No Harm ('87)
- ❑ ❑ 2 - Half a Mind ('90)

Maggie MacGowen
- ❏ ❏ 1 - Telling Lies ('92)
- ❏ ❏ 2 - Midnight Baby ('93)
- ❏ ❏ 3 - Bad Intent ('94)
- ❏ ❏ 4 - 77th Street Requiem ('95)

HOWE, Melodie Johnson
Claire Conrad & Maggie Hill
- ❏ ❏ 1 - The Mother Shadow ('89) ☆ ☆ ☆
- ❏ ❏ 2 - Beauty Dies ('94)

HUFF, Tanya
Vicki Nelson
- ❏ ❏ 1 - Blood Price ('92)
- ❏ ❏ 2 - Blood Trail ('92)
- ❏ ❏ 3 - Blood Lines ('93)
- ❏ ❏ 4 - Blood Pact ('93)

HUXLEY, Elspeth
Supt. Vachell
- ❏ ❏ 1 - Murder at Government House ('37)
- ❏ ❏ 2 - Murder on Safari ('38)
- ❏ ❏ 3 - The African Poison Murders ('39)
  [Britain-Death of an Aryan]

HYDE, Eleanor
Lydia Miller
- ❏ ❏ 1 - In Murder We Trust ('95)

J

JACKSON, Marian J. A.
Abigail Patience Danforth
- ❏ ❏ 1 - The Punjat's Ruby ('90)
- ❏ ❏ 2 - The Arabian Pearl ('90)
- ❏ ❏ 3 - Cat's Eye ('91)
- ❏ ❏ 4 - Diamond Head ('92)
- ❏ ❏ 5 - The Sunken Treasure ('94)

JACKSON, Muriel Resnick
Merrie Lee Spencer
- ❏ ❏ 1 - The Garden Club ('92)

JACOBS, Jonnie

Kali O'Brien
- ❏ ❏ 1 - Shadow of Doubt ('96)

Kate Austen
- ❏ ❏ 1 - Murder Among Neighbors ('94)
- ❏ ❏ 2 - Murder Among Friends ('95)

JACOBS, Nancy Baker

Devon MacDonald
- ❏ ❏ 1 - The Turquoise Tattoo ('91)
- ❏ ❏ 2 - A Slash of Scarlet ('92)
- ❏ ❏ 3 - The Silver Scalpel ('93)

JAFFE, Jody

Natalie Gold
- ❏ ❏ 1 - Horse of a Different Killer ('95)
- ❏ ❏ 2 - Chestnut Mare, Beware ('96)

JAMES, P. D. 🅿

Adam Dalgleish
- ❏ ❏ 1 - Cover Her Face ('62)
- ❏ ❏ 2 - A Mind to Murder ('63)
- ❏ ❏ 3 - Unnatural Causes ('67)
- ❏ ❏ 4 - Shroud for a Nightingale ('71) ★ ☆
- ❏ ❏ 5 - The Black Tower ('75) ★
- ❏ ❏ 6 - Death of an Expert Witness ('77)
- ❏ ❏ 7 - A Taste for Death ('86) ★ ★
- ❏ ❏ 8 - Devices and Desires ('89)
- ❏ ❏ 9 - Original Sin ('94)

Cordelia Gray
- ❏ ❏ 1 - An Unsuitable Job for a Woman ('72) ☆
- ❏ ❏ 2 - The Skull Beneath the Skin ('82)

JANCE, J. A.

J. P. Beaumont
- ❏ ❏ 1 - Until Proven Guilty ('85)
- ❏ ❏ 2 - Injustice for All ('86)
- ❏ ❏ 3 - Trial by Fury ('86)
- ❏ ❏ 4 - Taking the Fifth ('87)
- ❏ ❏ 5 - Improbable Cause ('88)
- ❏ ❏ 6 - A More Perfect Union ('88)
- ❏ ❏ 7 - Dismissed with Prejudice ('89)
- ❏ ❏ 8 - Minor in Possession ('90)
- ❏ ❏ 9 - Payment in Kind ('91)
- ❏ ❏ 10 - Without Due Process ('92) ★

❏ ❏ 11 - Failure to Appear ('93) ★
❏ ❏ 12 - Lying in Wait ('94)
❏ ❏ 13 - Name Withheld ('95)

Joanna Brady
❏ ❏ 1 - Desert Heat ('93)
❏ ❏ 2 - Tombstone Courage ('94)
❏ ❏ 3 - Shoot, Don't Shoot ('95)

JOHNS, Veronica Parker
Agatha Welch
❏ ❏ 1 - Hush, Gabriel! ('40)
❏ ❏ 2 - Shady Doings ('41)
Webster Flagg
❏ ❏ 1 - Murder by the Day ('53)
❏ ❏ 2 - Servant's Problem ('58)

JONES, Hazel Wynn
Emma Shaw
❏ ❏ 1 - Death and the Trumpets of Tuscany ('88)
❏ ❏ 2 - Shot on Locations ('90)

JORDAN, Jennifer
Barry & Dee Vaughan
❏ ❏ 1 - A Good Weekend for Murder ('87)
❏ ❏ 2 - Murder Under the Mistletoe ('88)
❏ ❏ 3 - Book Early for Murder ('90)
Kristin Ashe
❏ ❏ 1 - A Safe Place to Sleep ('92)
❏ ❏ 2 - Existing Solutions ('93)

JORGENSEN, Christine T.
Stella the Stargazer
❏ ❏ 1 - A Love to Die For ('94)
❏ ❏ 2 - You Bet Your Life ('95)

✦ 𝒦 ✦

KALLEN, Lucille
Maggie Rome & C. B. Greenfield
❏ ❏ 1 - Introducing C. B. Greenfield ('79)
❏ ❏ 2 - The Tanglewood Murder ('80)
❏ ❏ 3 - No Lady in the House ('82)
❏ ❏ 4 - The Piano Bird ('84)
❏ ❏ 5 - A Little Madness ('86)

KARR, Leona
Addie Devore
- ❏ ❏ 1 - Murder in Bandora ('93)

KELLERMAN, Faye
Peter Decker & Rina Lazarus
- ❏ ❏ 1 - The Ritual Bath ('86) ★
- ❏ ❏ 2 - Sacred and Profane ('87)
- ❏ ❏ 3 - Milk and Honey ('90)
- ❏ ❏ 4 - Day of Atonement ('92)
- ❏ ❏ 5 - False Prophet ('92)
- ❏ ❏ 6 - Grievous Sin ('93)
- ❏ ❏ 7 - Sanctuary ('94)
- ❏ ❏ 8 - Justice ('95)

KELLY, Mary
Brett Nightingale
- ❏ ❏ 1 - A Cold Coming ('56)
- ❏ ❏ 2 - Dead Man's Riddle ('57)
- ❏ ❏ 3 - The Christmas Egg ('58)

Hedley Nicholson
- ❏ ❏ 1 - The Spoilt Kill ('61) ★
- ❏ ❏ 2 - Due to a Death ('62)
         [U.S.-The Dead of Summer]

KELLY, Mary Ann
Claire Breslinsky
- ❏ ❏ 1 - Parklane South, Queens ('90)
- ❏ ❏ 2 - Foxglove ('92)

KELLY, Nora
Gillian Adams
- ❏ ❏ 1 - In the Shadow of King's ('84)
- ❏ ❏ 2 - My Sister's Keeper ('92)
- ❏ ❏ 3 - Bad Chemistry ('93)

KELLY, Susan
Liz Connors
- ❏ ❏ 1 - The Gemini Man ('85) ☆
- ❏ ❏ 2 - The Summertime Soldiers ('86)
- ❏ ❏ 3 - Trail of the Dragon ('88)
- ❏ ❏ 4 - Until Proven Innocent ('90)
- ❏ ❏ 5 - And Soon I'll Come to Kill You ('91)
- ❏ ❏ 6 - Out of the Darkness ('92)

KELLY, Susan B.
Alison Hope & Nick Trevellyan
- ❏ ❏ 1 - Hope Against Hope ('90)
- ❏ ❏ 2 - Time of Hope ('90)
- ❏ ❏ 3 - Hope Will Answer ('93)
- ❏ ❏ 4 - Kid's Stuff ('94)

KELNER, Toni L. P.
Laura Fleming
- ❏ ❏ 1 - Down Home Murder ('93)
- ❏ ❏ 2 - Dead Ringer ('94)
- ❏ ❏ 3 - Trouble Looking for a Place to Happen ('95)

KENNEY, Susan
Roz Howard & Alan Stewart
- ❏ ❏ 1 - Garden of Malice ('83)
- ❏ ❏ 2 - Graves of Academe ('85)
- ❏ ❏ 3 - One Fell Sloop ('90)

KIJEWSKI, Karen
Kat Colorado
- ❏ ❏ 1 - Katwalk ('88) ★ ★ ★
- ❏ ❏ 2 - Katapult ('90)
- ❏ ❏ 3 - Kat's Cradle ('91)
- ❏ ❏ 4 - Copy Kat ('92)
- ❏ ❏ 5 - Wild Kat ('94)
- ❏ ❏ 6 - Alley Cat Blues ('95)

KING, Laurie R.
Kate Martinelli & Alonzo Hawkin
- ❏ ❏ 1 - A Grave Talent ('93) ★ ☆
- ❏ ❏ 2 - To Play the Fool ('95)
- ❏ ❏ 3 - With Child ('96)
Mary Russell
- ❏ ❏ 1 - The Beekeeper's Apprentice ('94) ☆
- ❏ ❏ 2 - A Monstrous Regiment of Women ('95)

KINGSBURY, Kate 🅿
Cecily Sinclair
- ❏ ❏ 1 - Room with a Clue ('93)
- ❏ ❏ 2 - Do Not Disturb ('94)
- ❏ ❏ 3 - Service for Two ('94)
- ❏ ❏ 4 - Eat, Drink, and Be Buried ('94)
- ❏ ❏ 5 - Check-out Time ('95)
- ❏ ❏ 6 - Grounds for Murder ('95)

KITTREDGE, Mary

Charlotte Kent
- ❏ ❏ 1 - Murder in Mendocino ('87)
- ❏ ❏ 2 - Dead and Gone ('89)
- ❏ ❏ 3 - Poison Pen ('90)

Edwina Crusoe
- ❏ ❏ 1 - Fatal Diagnosis ('90)
- ❏ ❏ 2 - Rigor Mortis ('91)
- ❏ ❏ 3 - Cadaver ('92)
- ❏ ❏ 4 - Walking Dead Man ('92)
- ❏ ❏ 5 - Desperate Remedy ('93)
- ❏ ❏ 6 - Kill or Cure ('95)

KNIGHT, Alanna

Jeremy Faro
- ❏ ❏ 1 - Enter Second Murderer ('88)
- ❏ ❏ 2 - Bloodline ('89)
- ❏ ❏ 3 - Deadly Beloved ('89)
- ❏ ❏ 4 - Killing Cousins ('90)
- ❏ ❏ 5 - A Quiet Death ('91)
- ❏ ❏ 6 - To Kill a Queen ('92)
- ❏ ❏ 7 - The Evil That Men Do ('93)
- ❏ ❏ 8 - The Missing Duchess ('94)

KNIGHT, Kathleen Moore

Elisha Macomber
- ❏ ❏ 1 - Death Blew Out the Match ('35)
- ❏ ❏ 2 - The Wheel That Turned ('36)
  [APA–Murder Greets Jean Holton]
- ❏ ❏ 3 - The Clue of the Poor Man's Shilling ('36)
  [Britain-The Poor Man's Shilling]
- ❏ ❏ 4 - Seven Were Veiled ('37)
  [Britain-Seven Were Suspect]
  [APA–Death Wears a ('Bridal) Veil]
- ❏ ❏ 5 - The Tainted Token ('38)
  [APA–The Case of the Tainted Token]
- ❏ ❏ 6 - Acts of Black Night ('38)
- ❏ ❏ 7 - Death Came Dancing ('40)
- ❏ ❏ 8 - The Trouble at Turkey Hill ('46)
- ❏ ❏ 9 - Footbridge to Death ('47)
- ❏ ❏ 10 - Bait for Murder ('48)
- ❏ ❏ 11 - The Bass Derby Murder ('49)
- ❏ ❏ 12 - Death Goes to a Reunion ('52)
- ❏ ❏ 13 - Akin to Murder ('53)
- ❏ ❏ 14 - Three of Diamonds ('53)

❑ ❑ 15 - Valse Macabre ('54)
❑ ❑ 16 - Beauty Is a Beast ('59)
Margot Blair
❑ ❑ 1 - Rendezvous with the Past ('40)
❑ ❑ 2 - Exit a Star ('41)
❑ ❑ 3 - Terror by Twilight ('42)
❑ ❑ 4 - Design in Diamonds ('44)

KNIGHT, Kathryn Lasky
Calista Jacobs
❑ ❑ 1 - Trace Elements ('86)
❑ ❑ 2 - Mortal Words ('90)
❑ ❑ 3 - Mumbo Jumbo ('91)
❑ ❑ 4 - Dark Swain ('94)

KNIGHT, Phyllis
Lil Ritchie
❑ ❑ 1 - Switching the Odds ('92) ☆
❑ ❑ 2 - Shattered Rhythms ('94)
❑ ❑ 3 - Lost to Sight ('96)

KOMO, Dolores
Clio Browne
❑ ❑ 1 - Clio Browne: Private Investigator ('88)

KRAFT, Gabrielle
Jerry Zalman
❑ ❑ 1 - Bullshot ('87) ☆
❑ ❑ 2 - Screwdriver ('88)
❑ ❑ 3 - Let's Rob Roy ('89)
❑ ❑ 4 - Bloody Mary ('90)

KREUTER, Katherine E.
Paige Taylor
❑ ❑ 1 - Fool Me Once ('94)

KRICH, Rochelle Majer
Jessie Drake
❑ ❑ 1 - Fair Game ('93) ☆
❑ ❑ 2 - Angel of Death ('94) ☆
❑ ❑ 3 - Speak No Evil ('96)

KRUGER, Mary
Brooke Cassidy & Matt Devlin
❑ ❑ 1 - Death on the Cliff Walk ('94)

KUNZ, Kathleen
Terry Girard
- ❑ ❑ 1 - Murder Once Removed ('93)
- ❑ ❑ 2 - Death in a Private Place ('96)

━━━━━━━━━━━ *L* ━━━━━━━━━━━

LACEY, Sarah 🅿
Leah Hunter
- ❑ ❑ 1 - File Under: Deceased ('92)
- ❑ ❑ 2 - File Under: Missing ('93)
- ❑ ❑ 3 - File Under: Arson ('94)
- ❑ ❑ 4 - File Under: Jeopardy ('95)

LACHNIT, Carroll
Hannah Barlow
- ❑ ❑ 1 - Murder in Brief ('95)
- ❑ ❑ 2 - A Blessed Death ('96)

LACKEY, Mercedes
Diana Tregarde
- ❑ ❑ 1 - Burning Water ('89)
- ❑ ❑ 2 - Children of the Night ('90)
- ❑ ❑ 3 - Jinx High ('91)

LAMB, J. Dayne
Teal Stewart
- ❑ ❑ 1 - Questionable Behavior ('93)
- ❑ ❑ 2 - A Question of Preference ('94)
- ❑ ❑ 3 - Unquestioned Loyalty ('95)

LAMBERT, Mercedes
Whitney Logan
- ❑ ❑ 1 - Dogtown ('91)

LANDRETH, Marsha
Dr. Samantha Turner
- ❑ ❑ 1 - The Holiday Murders ('92)
- ❑ ❑ 2 - A Clinic for Murder ('93)
- ❑ ❑ 3 - Vial Murders ('95)

 What award-winning private eye writer and former Hollywood screenwriter is the daughter of a Kentucky attorney who also wrote mysteries?

LANGTON, Jane
Homer Kelly
- ❑ ❑ 1 - The Transcendental Murder ('64)
  [APA–The Minuteman Murder ('76)]
- ❑ ❑ 2 - Dark Nantucket Noon ('75)
- ❑ ❑ 3 - The Memorial Hall Murder ('78)
- ❑ ❑ 4 - Natural Enemy ('82)
- ❑ ❑ 5 - Emily Dickinson Is Dead ('84) ☆
- ❑ ❑ 6 - Good and Dead ('86)
- ❑ ❑ 7 - Murder at the Gardner ('88)
- ❑ ❑ 8 - The Dante Game ('91)
- ❑ ❑ 9 - God in Concord ('92)
- ❑ ❑ 10 - Divine Inspiration ('93)
- ❑ ❑ 11 - The Shortest Day ('95)

LA PIERRE, Janet
Vince Gutierrez & Meg Halloran
- ❑ ❑ 1 - Unquiet Grave ('87) ☆
- ❑ ❑ 2 - Children's Games ('89)
- ❑ ❑ 3 - Cruel Mother ('90)
- ❑ ❑ 4 - Grandmother's House ('91)
- ❑ ❑ 5 - Old Enemies ('93) ☆

LA PLANTE, Lynda
Dolly Rawlins
- ❑ ❑ 1 - The Widows ('83)
- ❑ ❑ 2 - The Widows II ('85)
Jane Tennison
- ❑ ❑ 1 - Prime Suspect ('93)
- ❑ ❑ 2 - Prime Suspect 2 ('93)
- ❑ ❑ 3 - Prime Suspect 3 ('94)

LATHEN, Emma 🄿
John Putnam Thatcher
- ❑ ❑ 1 - Banking on Death ('61)
- ❑ ❑ 2 - A Place for Murder ('63)
- ❑ ❑ 3 - Accounting for Murder ('64) ★
- ❑ ❑ 4 - Murder Makes the Wheels Go 'Round ('66)
- ❑ ❑ 5 - Death Shall Overcome ('66)
- ❑ ❑ 6 - Murder Against the Grain ('67) ★
- ❑ ❑ 7 - A Stitch in Time ('68)
- ❑ ❑ 8 - Come to Dust ('68)
- ❑ ❑ 9 - When in Greece ('69) ☆
- ❑ ❑ 10 - Murder to Go ('69)
- ❑ ❑ 11 - Pick Up Sticks ('70)

❑ ❑ 12 - Ashes to Ashes ('71)
❑ ❑ 13 - The Longer the Thread ('71)
❑ ❑ 14 - Murder Without Icing ('72)
❑ ❑ 15 - Sweet and Low ('74)
❑ ❑ 16 - By Hook or By Crook ('75)
❑ ❑ 17 - Double, Double, Oil and Trouble ('78)
❑ ❑ 18 - Going for the Gold ('81)
❑ ❑ 19 - Green Grow the Dollars ('82) ★
❑ ❑ 20 - Something in the Air ('88)
❑ ❑ 21 - East Is East ('91)
❑ ❑ 22 - Right on the Money ('93)

LAURENCE, Janet
Darina Lisle
❑ ❑ 1 - A Deepe Coffyn ('89)
❑ ❑ 2 - A Tasty Way to Die ('90)
❑ ❑ 3 - Hotel Morgue ('91)
❑ ❑ 4 - Recipe for Death ('92)
❑ ❑ 5 - Death and the Epicure ('93)
❑ ❑ 6 - Death at the Table ('94)
❑ ❑ 7 - Death a la Provencale ('95)

LAW, Janice
Anna Peters
❑ ❑ 1 - The Big Pay-off ('76) ☆
❑ ❑ 2 - Gemini Trip ('77)
❑ ❑ 3 - Under Orion ('78)
❑ ❑ 4 - The Shadow of the Palms ('80)
❑ ❑ 5 - Death Under Par ('81)
❑ ❑ 6 - Time Lapse ('92)
❑ ❑ 7 - A Safe Place to Die ('93)
❑ ❑ 8 - Backfire ('94)

LAWRENCE, Hilda
Mark East, Bessie Petty & Beulah Pond
❑ ❑ 1 - Blood Upon the Snow ('44)
❑ ❑ 2 - A Time to Die ('44)
❑ ❑ 3 - Death of a Doll ('47)

LAWRENCE, Martha
Dr. Elizabeth Chase
❑ ❑ 1 - Murder in Scorpio ('95)

LEE, Barbara
Eve Elliott
❑ ❑ 1 - Death in Still Waters ('95) ★

LEE, Marie
Marguerite Smith
- ☐ ☐ 1 - The Curious Cape Cod Skull ('95)

LEE, W. W. (Wendi)
Jefferson Birch
- ☐ ☐ 1 - Rogue's Gold ('89)
- ☐ ☐ 2 - Rustler's Venom ('90)
- ☐ ☐ 3 - Rancher's Blood ('91)
- ☐ ☐ 4 - Robber's Trail ('92)
- ☐ ☐ 5 - Outlaw's Fortune ('93)
- ☐ ☐ 6 - Cannon's Revenge ('95)

Angela Matelli
- ☐ ☐ 1 - The Good Daughter ('94)

LEEK, Margaret 🄿
Stephen Marryat
- ☐ ☐ 1 - We Must Have a Trial ('80)
- ☐ ☐ 2 - The Healthy Grave ('80)
- ☐ ☐ 3 - Voice of the Past ('81)

LEMARCHAND, Elizabeth
Tom Pollard & Gregory Toye
- ☐ ☐ 1 - Death of an Old Girl ('67)
- ☐ ☐ 2 - The Affacombe Affair ('68)
- ☐ ☐ 3 - Alibi for a Corpse ('69)
- ☐ ☐ 4 - Death on Doomsday ('71)
- ☐ ☐ 5 - Cyanide with Compliments ('72)
- ☐ ☐ 6 - Let or Hindrance ('73)
  [U.S.-No Vacation from Murder]
- ☐ ☐ 7 - Buried in the Past ('74)
- ☐ ☐ 8 - Step in the Dark ('76)
- ☐ ☐ 9 - Unhappy Returns ('77)
- ☐ ☐ 10 - Suddenly While Gardening ('78)
- ☐ ☐ 11 - Change for the Worse ('80)
- ☐ ☐ 12 - Nothing to do with the Case ('81)
- ☐ ☐ 13 - Troubled Waters ('82)
- ☐ ☐ 14 - The Wheel Turns ('83)
- ☐ ☐ 15 - Light through the Glass ('84)
- ☐ ☐ 16 - Who Goes Home? ('86)
- ☐ ☐ 17 - The Glade Manor Murder ('88)

? What *Essence* magazine editor has created a single-mother private eye from Newark?

LEON, Donna
Guido Brunetti
❑ ❑ 1 - Death at la Fenice ('92)
❑ ❑ 2 - Death in a Strange Country ('93)
❑ ❑ 3 - Dressed for Death ('94)
  [Britain-The Anonymous Venetian]
❑ ❑ 4 - Death and Judgment ('95)
  [APA–A Venetian Reckoning]

LEONARD, Charles L. 🅿
Paul Kilgerrin
❑ ❑ 1 - The Stolen Squadron ('42)
❑ ❑ 2 - Deadline for Destruction ('42)
❑ ❑ 3 - The Fanatic of Fez ('43)
  [APA–Assignment to Death]
❑ ❑ 4 - The Secret of the Spa ('44)
❑ ❑ 5 - Expert in Murder ('45)
❑ ❑ 6 - Pursuit in Peru ('46)
❑ ❑ 7 - Search for a Scientist ('48)
❑ ❑ 8 - The Fourth Funeral ('48)
❑ ❑ 9 - Sinister Shelter ('49)
❑ ❑ 10 - Secrets for Sale ('50)
❑ ❑ 11 - Treachery in Trieste ('51)

LEWIS, Sherry
Fred Vickery
❑ ❑ 1 - No Place for Secrets ('95)

LININGTON, Elizabeth
Sgt. Ivor Maddox
❑ ❑ 1 - Greenmask! ('64)
❑ ❑ 2 - No Evil Angel ('64)
❑ ❑ 3 - Date with Death ('66)
❑ ❑ 4 - Something Wrong ('67)
❑ ❑ 5 - Policeman's Lot ('68)
❑ ❑ 6 - Practice to Deceive ('71)
❑ ❑ 7 - Crime by Chance ('73)
❑ ❑ 8 - Perchance of Death ('77)
❑ ❑ 9 - No Villian Need Be ('79)
❑ ❑ 10 - Consequence of Crime ('80)
❑ ❑ 11 - Skeletons in the Closet ('82)
❑ ❑ 12 - Felony Report ('84)
❑ ❑ 13 - Strange Felony ('86)

LINSCOTT, Gillian

Birdie Linnet
- ❏ ❏ 1 - A Healthy Body ('84)
- ❏ ❏ 2 - Murder Makes Tracks ('85)
- ❏ ❏ 3 - A Whiff of Sulphur ('87)

Nell Bray
- ❏ ❏ 1 - Sister Beneath the Sheet ('91)
- ❏ ❏ 2 - Hanging on the Wire ('92)
- ❏ ❏ 3 - Stage Fright ('93)
- ❏ ❏ 4 - An Easy Day for a Lady ('94)
  [Britain-Widow's Peak]

LIVINGSTON, Nancy

G. D. H. Pringle
- ❏ ❏ 1 - The Trouble at Aquitaine ('85)
- ❏ ❏ 2 - Fatality at Bath & Wells ('86)
- ❏ ❏ 3 - Incident at Parva ('87)
- ❏ ❏ 4 - Death in a Distant Land ('88)
- ❏ ❏ 5 - Death in Close-up ('89)
- ❏ ❏ 6 - Mayhem at Parva ('90)

LOCKRIDGE, Frances & Richard

Insp. Merton Heimrich
- ❏ ❏ 1 - Think of Death ('47)
- ❏ ❏ 2 - I Want to Go Home ('48)
- ❏ ❏ 3 - Spin Your Web, Lady! ('49)
- ❏ ❏ 4 - Foggy, Foggy Death ('50)
- ❏ ❏ 5 - A Client Is Cancelled ('51)
- ❏ ❏ 6 - Death by Association ('52)
- ❏ ❏ 7 - Stand Up and Die ('52)
- ❏ ❏ 8 - Death and the Gentle Bull ('54)
- ❏ ❏ 9 - Burnt Offering ('55)
- ❏ ❏ 10 - Let Dead Enough Alone ('56)
- ❏ ❏ 11 - Practice to Deceive ('57)
- ❏ ❏ 12 - Accent on Murder ('58)
- ❏ ❏ 13 - Show Red for Danger ('60)
- ❏ ❏ 14 - With One Stone ('61)
- ❏ ❏ 15 - First Come, First Kill ('62)
- ❏ ❏ 16 - The Distant Clue ('63)
- ❏ ❏ 17 - Murder Can't Wait ('64)
- ❏ ❏ 18 - Murder Roundabout ('66)
- ❏ ❏ 19 - With Option to Die ('67)
- ❏ ❏ 20 - A Risky Way to Kill ('69)
- ❏ ❏ 21 - Inspector's Holiday ('71)
- ❏ ❏ 22 - Not I, Said the Sparrow ('73)

❑ ❑ 23 - Dead Run ('76)
❑ ❑ 24 - The Tenth Life ('77)

Pam & Jerry North
❑ ❑ 1 - The Norths Meet Murder ('40)
❑ ❑ 2 - Murder Out of Turn ('41)
❑ ❑ 3 - A Pinch of Poison ('41)
❑ ❑ 4 - Death on the Aisle ('42)
❑ ❑ 5 - Hanged for a Sheep ('42)
❑ ❑ 6 - Death Takes a Bow ('43)
❑ ❑ 7 - Killing the Goose ('44)
❑ ❑ 8 - Payoff for the Banker ('45)
❑ ❑ 9 - Death of a Tall Man ('46)
❑ ❑ 10 - Murder Within Murder ('46)
❑ ❑ 11 - Untidy Murder ('47)
❑ ❑ 12 - Murder Is Served ('48)
❑ ❑ 13 - The Dishonest Murder ('49)
❑ ❑ 14 - Murder in a Hurry ('50)
❑ ❑ 15 - Murder Comes First ('51)
❑ ❑ 16 - Dead as a Dinosaur ('52)
❑ ❑ 17 - Death Has a Small Voice ('53)
❑ ❑ 18 - Curtain for a Jester ('53)
❑ ❑ 19 - A Key to Death ('54)
❑ ❑ 20 - Death of an Angel ('55)
❑ ❑ 21 - Voyage into Violence ('56)
❑ ❑ 22 - The Long Skeleton ('58)
❑ ❑ 23 - Murder Is Suggested ('59)
❑ ❑ 24 - The Judge Is Reversed ('60)
❑ ❑ 25 - Murder Has Its Points ('61)
❑ ❑ 26 - Murder by the Book ('63)

LOGAN, Margaret
Olivia Chapman
❑ ❑ 1 - The End of an Altruist ('94)
❑ ❑ 2 - Never Let a Stranger in Your House ('95)

LOGUE, Mary
Laura Malloy
❑ ❑ 1 - Still Explosion ('93)

LORDEN, Randye
Sydney Sloane
❑ ❑ 1 - Brotherly Love ('93) ☆
❑ ❑ 2 - Sister's Keeper ('94)

LORENS, M. K. 🅿
William Marlowe Sherman
- ❏ ❏ 1 - Sweet Narcissus ('90)
- ❏ ❏ 2 - Ropedancer's Fall ('90)
- ❏ ❏ 3 - Deception Island ('91)
- ❏ ❏ 4 - Dreamland ('92)
- ❏ ❏ 5 - Sorrowheart ('93)

LOVETT, Sarah
Dr. Sylvia Strange
- ❏ ❏ 1 - Dangerous Attachments ('95)
- ❏ ❏ 2 - Acquired Motive ('96)

LUCKE, Margaret
Jessica Randolph
- ❏ ❏ 1 - A Relative Stranger ('91)
- ❏ ❏ 2 - Bridge to Nowhere ('96)

LYONS, Nan & Ivan
Natasha O'Brien & Millie Ogden
- ❏ ❏ 1 - Someone Is Killing the Great Chefs of Europe ('76)
- ❏ ❏ 2 - Someone Is Killing the Great Chefs of America ('93)

▒▒▒▒▒▒▒▒▒▒▒▒ *M* ▒▒▒▒▒▒▒▒▒▒▒▒

MACGREGOR, T. J.
Quin St. James & Mike McCleary
- ❏ ❏ 1 - Dark Fields ('86) ☆
- ❏ ❏ 2 - Kill Flash ('87)
- ❏ ❏ 3 - Death Sweet ('88)
- ❏ ❏ 4 - On Ice ('89)
- ❏ ❏ 5 - Kin Dread ('90)
- ❏ ❏ 6 - Death Flats ('91)
- ❏ ❏ 7 - Spree ('92)
- ❏ ❏ 8 - Storm Surge ('93)
- ❏ ❏ 9 - Blue Pearl ('94)
- ❏ ❏ 10 - Mistress of the Bones ('95)

MACKAY, Amanda
Hannah Land
- ❏ ❏ 1 - Murder Is Academic ('76)
- ❏ ❏ 2 - Death on the Eno ('81)

MACLEOD, Charlotte
Peter Shandy & Helen Marsh Shandy
- ❏ ❏ 1 - Rest You Merry ('78)
- ❏ ❏ 2 - The Luck Runs Out ('79)
- ❏ ❏ 3 - Wrack and Rune ('82)
- ❏ ❏ 4 - Something the Cat Dragged In ('83)
- ❏ ❏ 5 - The Curse of the Giant Hogweed ('85)
- ❏ ❏ 6 - The Corpse in Oozak's Pond ('86) ☆
- ❏ ❏ 7 - Vane Pursuit ('89)
- ❏ ❏ 8 - An Owl Too Many ('91) ☆
- ❏ ❏ 9 - Something in the Water ('94)

Sarah Kelling & Max Bittersohn
- ❏ ❏ 1 - The Family Vault ('79)
- ❏ ❏ 2 - The Withdrawing Room ('80)
- ❏ ❏ 3 - The Palace Guard ('81)
- ❏ ❏ 4 - The Bilbao Looking Glass ('83)
- ❏ ❏ 5 - The Convivial Codfish ('84)
- ❏ ❏ 6 - The Plain Old Man ('85)
- ❏ ❏ 7 - The Silver Ghost ('87)
- ❏ ❏ 8 - The Recycled Citizen ('87)
- ❏ ❏ 9 - The Gladstone Bag ('89)
- ❏ ❏ 10 - The Resurrection Man ('92)
- ❏ ❏ 11 - The Odd Job ('95)

MAIMAN, Jaye
Robin Miller
- ❏ ❏ 1 - I Left My Heart ('91)
- ❏ ❏ 2 - Crazy for Loving ('92) ★
- ❏ ❏ 3 - Under My Skin ('93)
- ❏ ❏ 4 - Someone to Watch ('95)

MALMONT, Valerie S.
Tori Miracle
- ❏ ❏ 1 - Death Pays the Rose Rent ('94)

MANEY, Mabel
Nancy Clue
- ❏ ❏ 1 - The Case of the Not-So-Nice Nurse ('93)
- ❏ ❏ 2 - The Case of the Good-for-Nothing Girlfriend ('94)
- ❏ ❏ 3 - The Ghost in the Closet ('95)

MANN, Jessica
Tamara Hoyland
- ❏ ❏ 1 - Funeral Sites ('82)
- ❏ ❏ 2 - No Man's Island ('83)
- ❏ ❏ 3 - Grave Goods ('84)

❑ ❑ 4 - A Kind of Healthy Grave ('86)
❑ ❑ 5 - Death Beyond the Nile ('88)
❑ ❑ 6 - Faith, Hope and Homicide ('91)
Thea Crawford
❑ ❑ 1 - The Only Security ('72)
[U.S.-Troublecross]
❑ ❑ 2 - Captive Audience ('75)

MANTHORNE, Jackie
Harriett Hubley
❑ ❑ 1 - Ghost Motel ('94)
❑ ❑ 2 - Deadly Reunion ('95)

MARIZ, Linda French
Laura Ireland
❑ ❑ 1 - Body English ('92)
❑ ❑ 2 - Snake Dance ('92)

MARON, Margaret
Deborah Knott
❑ ❑ 1 - Bootlegger's Daughter ('92) ★ ★ ★ ★
❑ ❑ 2 - Southern Discomfort ('93) ☆ ☆
❑ ❑ 3 - Shooting at Loons ('94)
Sigrid Harald
❑ ❑ 1 - One Coffee With ('81)
❑ ❑ 2 - Death of a Butterfly ('84)
❑ ❑ 3 - Death in Blue Folders ('85)
❑ ❑ 4 - The Right Jack ('87)
❑ ❑ 5 - Baby Doll Games ('88)
❑ ❑ 6 - Corpus Christmas ('89) ☆ ☆
❑ ❑ 7 - Past Imperfect ('91)
❑ ❑ 8 - Fugitive Colors ('95)

MARSH, Ngaio
Roderick Alleyn
❑ ❑ 1 - A Man Lay Dead ('34)
❑ ❑ 2 - Enter a Murderer ('35)
❑ ❑ 3 - The Nursing-Home Murder ('35)
❑ ❑ 4 - Death in Ecstasy ('36)
❑ ❑ 5 - Vintage Murder ('37)
❑ ❑ 6 - Artists in Crime ('38)
❑ ❑ 7 - Death in a White Tie ('38)
❑ ❑ 8 - Overture to Death ('39)
❑ ❑ 9 - Death at the Bar ('40)
❑ ❑ 10 - Death of a Peer ('40)
[Britain-Surfeit of Lampreys]

❑ ❑ 11 - Death and the Dancing Footman ('41)
❑ ❑ 12 - Colour Scheme ('43)
❑ ❑ 13 - Died in the Wool ('45)
❑ ❑ 14 - Final Curtain ('47)
❑ ❑ 15 - Swing, Brother, Swing ('49)
     [U.S.-A Wreath for Rivera]
❑ ❑ 16 - Opening Night ('51)
     [U.S.-Night at the Vulcan]
❑ ❑ 17 - Spinsters in Jeopardy ('53)
     [APA–The Bride of Death]
❑ ❑ 18 - Scales of Justice ('55) ★
❑ ❑ 19 - Death of a Fool ('56)
     [Britain-Off with His Head]
❑ ❑ 20 - Singing in the Shrouds ('58)
❑ ❑ 21 - False Scent ('59)
❑ ❑ 22 - Hand in Glove ('62)
❑ ❑ 23 - Dead Water ('63)
❑ ❑ 24 - Killer Dolphin ('66) ☆
     [Britain-Death at the Dolphin]
❑ ❑ 25 - Clutch of Constables ('68)
❑ ❑ 26 - When in Rome ('70)
❑ ❑ 27 - Tied up in Tinsel ('72) ☆
❑ ❑ 28 - Black as He's Painted ('74)
❑ ❑ 29 - Last Ditch ('77)
❑ ❑ 30 - Grave Mistake ('78)
❑ ❑ 31 - Photo-Finish ('80)
❑ ❑ 32 - Light Thickens ('82)

MARTIN, Lee 🄿
Deb Ralston
❑ ❑ 1 - Too Sane a Murder ('84)
❑ ❑ 2 - A Conspiracy of Strangers ('86)
❑ ❑ 3 - Death Warmed Over ('88)
❑ ❑ 4 - Murder at the Blue Owl ('88)
❑ ❑ 5 - Hal's Own Murder Case ('89)
❑ ❑ 6 - Deficit Ending ('90)
❑ ❑ 7 - The Mensa Murders ('90)
❑ ❑ 8 - Hacker ('92)
❑ ❑ 9 - The Day That Dusty Died ('93)
❑ ❑ 10 - Inherited Murder ('94)
❑ ❑ 11 - Bird in a Cage ('95)

 Name the husband and wife collaborators who write a history-mystery series starring an American author of penny dreadfuls.

MASON, Sarah Jill
D. S. Trewley and Sgt. Stone
- ❑ ❑ 1 - Murder in the Maze ('93)
- ❑ ❑ 2 - Frozen Stiff ('93)
- ❑ ❑ 3 - Corpse in the Kitchen ('94)
- ❑ ❑ 4 - Dying Breath ('94)

MATERA, Lia
Laura Di Palma
- ❑ ❑ 1 - The Smart Money ('88)
- ❑ ❑ 2 - The Good Fight ('90)
- ❑ ❑ 3 - A Hard Bargain ('92)
- ❑ ❑ 4 - Face Value ('94)
- ❑ ❑ 5 - Designer Crimes ('95)

Willa Jansson
- ❑ ❑ 1 - Where Lawyers Fear to Tread ('86) ☆
- ❑ ❑ 2 - A Radical Departure ('87) ☆
- ❑ ❑ 3 - Hidden Agenda ('89)
- ❑ ❑ 4 - Prior Convictions ('91) ☆
- ❑ ❑ 5 - Last Chants ('96)

MATHER, Linda
Jo Hughes
- ❑ ❑ 1 - Blood of an Aries ('94)
- ❑ ❑ 2 - Beware Taurus ('94)

MATHEWS, Francine
Meredith "Merry" Folger
- ❑ ❑ 1 - Death in the Off-Season ('94)
- ❑ ❑ 2 - Death in Rough Water ('95)

MATTESON, Stefanie
Charlotte Graham
- ❑ ❑ 1 - Murder at the Spa ('90)
- ❑ ❑ 2 - Murder on the Cliff ('91)
- ❑ ❑ 3 - Murder at Teatime ('91)
- ❑ ❑ 4 - Murder on the Silk Road ('92)
- ❑ ❑ 5 - Murder at the Falls ('93)
- ❑ ❑ 6 - Murder on High ('94)

MATTHEWS, Alex
Cassidy McCabe
- ❑ ❑ 1 - Secret's Shadow ('96)
- ❑ ❑ 2 - Satan's Silence ('97)

MAXWELL, A. E. 🅿
Fiddler & Fiora Flynn
- ❏ ❏ 1 - Just Another Day in Paradise ('85)
- ❏ ❏ 2 - The Frog and the Scorpion ('86)
- ❏ ❏ 3 - Gatsby's Vineyard ('87)
- ❏ ❏ 4 - Just Enough Light to Kill ('88)
- ❏ ❏ 5 - The Art of Survival ('89)
- ❏ ❏ 6 - Money Burns ('91)
- ❏ ❏ 7 - The King of Nothing ('92)
- ❏ ❏ 8 - Murder Hurts ('93)

MCALLESTER, Melanie
Elizabeth Mendoza & Ashley Johnson
- ❏ ❏ 1 - The Lessons ('94)

MCCAFFERTY, Taylor
Haskell Blevins
- ❏ ❏ 1 - Pet Peeves ('90)
- ❏ ❏ 2 - Ruffled Feathers ('92)
- ❏ ❏ 3 - Bed Bugs ('92)
- ❏ ❏ 4 - Thin Skins ('94)
- ❏ ❏ 5 - Hanky Panky ('95)

MCCLELLAN, Tierney 🅿
Schuyler Ridgway
- ❏ ❏ 1 - Heir Condition ('95)
- ❏ ❏ 2 - Closing Statement ('95)
- ❏ ❏ 3 - A Killing in Real Estate ('96)

MCCLENDON, Lise
Alix Thorssen
- ❏ ❏ 1 - The Bluejay Shaman ('94)
- ❏ ❏ 2 - Painted Truth ('95)

MCCLOY, Helen
Dr. Basil Willing
- ❏ ❏ 1 - Dance of Death ('38) ★
  [APA–Design for Dying]
- ❏ ❏ 2 - The Man in the Moonlight ('40)
- ❏ ❏ 3 - The Deadly Truth ('41)
- ❏ ❏ 4 - Who's Calling ('42)
- ❏ ❏ 5 - Cue for Murder ('42)
- ❏ ❏ 6 - The Goblin Market ('43)
- ❏ ❏ 7 - The One That Got Away ('45)
- ❏ ❏ 8 - Through a Glass Darkly ('50)

❑ ❑ 9 - Alias Basil Willing ('51)
❑ ❑ 10 - The Long Body ('55)
❑ ❑ 11 - Two-thirds of a Ghost ('56)
❑ ❑ 12 - Mr. Splitfoot ('68)
❑ ❑ 13 - Burn This ('80)

MCCONNELL, Vickie P.
Nyla Wade
❑ ❑ 1 - Mrs. Porter's Letter ('82)
❑ ❑ 2 - The Burnton Widows ('84)
❑ ❑ 3 - Double Daughter ('88)

MCCRUMB, Sharyn
Elizabeth MacPherson
❑ ❑ 1 - Sick of Shadows ('84)
❑ ❑ 2 - Lovely in her Bones ('85)
❑ ❑ 3 - Highland Laddie Gone ('86)
❑ ❑ 4 - Paying the Piper ('88) ☆ ☆
❑ ❑ 5 - The Windsor Knot ('90)
❑ ❑ 6 - Missing Susan ('91)
❑ ❑ 7 - MacPherson's Lament ('92)
❑ ❑ 8 - If I'd Killed Him When I Met Him ('95)
James Owen Mega
❑ ❑ 1 - Bimbos of the Death Sun ('88) ★ ☆
❑ ❑ 2 - Zombies of the Gene Pool ('92)
Spencer Arrowood
❑ ❑ 1 - If Ever I Return, Pretty Peggy-O ('90) ★ ☆
❑ ❑ 2 - The Hangman's Beautiful Daughter ('92) ☆ ☆ ☆
❑ ❑ 3 - She Walks These Hills ('94) ★ ☆

MCDERMID, Val
Kate Brannigan
❑ ❑ 1 - Dead Beat ('92)
❑ ❑ 2 - Kickback ('93)
❑ ❑ 3 - Crack Down ('94) ☆
❑ ❑ 4 - Clean Break ('95)
Lindsay Gordon
❑ ❑ 1 - Report for Murder ('87)
❑ ❑ 2 - Common Murder ('89)
❑ ❑ 3 - Final Option ('91)
❑ ❑ 4 - Union Jack ('93)

MCFALL, Patricia
Nora James
❑ ❑ 1 - Night Butterfly ('92)

MCGERR, Patricia
Selena Mead
- ❏ ❏ 1 - Is There a Traitor in the House ('64)
- ❏ ❏ 2 - Legacy of Danger ('70)

MCGIFFIN, Janet
Dr. Maxene St. Clair
- ❏ ❏ 1 - Emergency Murder ('92)
- ❏ ❏ 2 - Prescription for Death ('93)
- ❏ ❏ 3 - Elective Murder ('95)

MCGOWN, Jill
Chief Insp. Lloyd & Judy Hill
- ❏ ❏ 1 - A Perfect Match ('83)
- ❏ ❏ 2 - Murder at the Old Vicarage ('88)
- ❏ ❏ 3 - Gone to Her Death ('89)
- ❏ ❏ 4 - The Murders of Mrs. Austin & Mrs. Beale ('91)
- ❏ ❏ 5 - The Other Woman ('92)
- ❏ ❏ 6 - Murder Now and Then ('93)
- ❏ ❏ 7 - A Shred of Evidence ('95)

MCGUIRE, Christine
Kathryn Mackay
- ❏ ❏ 1 - Until Proven Guilty ('93)

MCKENNA, Bridget
Caley Burke
- ❏ ❏ 1 - Murder Beach ('93)
- ❏ ❏ 2 - Dead Ahead ('94) ☆
- ❏ ❏ 3 - Caught Dead ('95)

MCKERNAN, Victoria
Chicago Nordejoong
- ❏ ❏ 1 - Osprey Reef ('90)
- ❏ ❏ 2 - Point Deception ('92)
- ❏ ❏ 3 - Crooked Island ('94)

MCKEVETT, G. A.
Savannah Reid
- ❏ ❏ 1 - Just Desserts ('95)

MCNAB, Claire
Carol Ashton
- ❏ ❏ 1 - Lessons in Murder ('88)
  [APA–Silver Moon ('90)]
- ❏ ❏ 2 - Fatal Reunion ('89)

❑ ❑ 3 - Death Down Under ('90)
❑ ❑ 4 - Cop Out ('91)
❑ ❑ 5 - Dead Certain ('92)
      [APA—Off Key]
❑ ❑ 6 - Body Guard ('94)

MCQUILLAN, Karin
Jazz Jasper
❑ ❑ 1 - Deadly Safari ('90)
❑ ❑ 2 - Elephants' Graveyard ('93)
❑ ❑ 3 - The Cheetah Chase ('94)

MCSHEA, Susannah Hofman
Mildred Bennett & friends
❑ ❑ 1 - Hometown Heroes ('90)
❑ ❑ 2 - The Pumpkin Shell Wife ('92)
❑ ❑ 3 - Ladybug, Ladybug ('94)

MEEK, M. R. D.
Lennox Kemp
❑ ❑ 1 - With Flowers That Fell ('83)
❑ ❑ 2 - Hang the Consequences ('84)
❑ ❑ 3 - The Split Second ('85)
❑ ❑ 4 - In Remembrance of Rose ('86)
❑ ❑ 5 - A Worm of Doubt ('87)
❑ ❑ 6 - A Mouthful of Sand ('88)
❑ ❑ 7 - A Loose Connection ('89)
❑ ❑ 8 - This Blessed Plot ('90)
❑ ❑ 9 - Touch & Go ('93)

MEIER, Leslie
Lucy Stone
❑ ❑ 1 - Mail-Order Murder ('93)
❑ ❑ 2 - Tippy-Toe Murder ('94)

MELVILLE, Jennie 🄿
Charmian Daniels
❑ ❑ 1 - Come Home and Be Killed ('62)
❑ ❑ 2 - Burning Is a Substitute for Loving ('63)
❑ ❑ 3 - Murderer's Houses ('64)
❑ ❑ 4 - There Lies Your Love ('65)
❑ ❑ 5 - Nell Alone ('66)
❑ ❑ 6 - A Different Kind of Summer ('67)
❑ ❑ 7 - A New Kind of Killer ('70)
❑ ❑ 8 - Murder Has a Pretty Face ('81)
❑ ❑ 9 - Windsor Red ('88)

❑ ❑ 10 - Murder in the Garden ('89)
❑ ❑ 11 - Making Good Blood ('89)
❑ ❑ 12 - Witching Murder ('90)
❑ ❑ 13 - Dead Set ('93)
❑ ❑ 14 - Footsteps in the Blood ('93)
❑ ❑ 15 - Death in the Family ('94)
     [Britain-Baby Drop]

MEREDITH, D. R.
Charles Matthews
❑ ❑ 1 - The Sheriff & the Panhandle Murders ('84)
❑ ❑ 2 - The Sheriff & the Branding Iron Murders ('85)
❑ ❑ 3 - The Sheriff & the Folsom Man Murders ('87)
❑ ❑ 4 - The Sheriff & the Pheasant Hunt Murders ('93)
❑ ❑ 5 - The Homefront Murders ('95)

John Lloyd Branson & Lydia Fairchild
❑ ❑ 1 - Murder by Impulse ('88) ☆
❑ ❑ 2 - Murder by Deception ('89) ☆
❑ ❑ 3 - Murder by Masquerade ('90)
❑ ❑ 4 - Murder by Reference ('91)
❑ ❑ 5 - Murder by Sacrilege ('93)

MEYERS, Annette
Xenia Smith & Leslie Wetzon
❑ ❑ 1 - The Big Killing ('89)
❑ ❑ 2 - Tender Death ('90)
❑ ❑ 3 - The Deadliest Option ('91)
❑ ❑ 4 - Blood on the Street ('92)
❑ ❑ 5 - Murder: The Musical ('93)
❑ ❑ 6 - These Bones Were Made for Dancin' ('95)
❑ ❑ 7 - The Groaning Board ('97)

MEYERS, Maan 🅿
The Tonnemans
❑ ❑ 1 - The Dutchman ('92)
❑ ❑ 2 - The Kingsbridge Plot ('93)
❑ ❑ 3 - The High Constable ('94)
❑ ❑ 4 - The Dutchman's Dilemma ('95)

MICHAELS, Barbara 🅿
Georgetown house
❑ ❑ 1 - Ammie, Come Home ('68)
❑ ❑ 2 - Shattered Silk ('86)
❑ ❑ 3 - Stitches in Time ('95)

MICKELBURY, Penny
Gianna Maglione & Mimi Patterson
- ❑ ❑ 1 - Keeping Secrets ('94)
- ❑ ❑ 2 - Night Songs ('95)

MILLAR, Margaret
Insp. Sands
- ❑ ❑ 1 - Wall of Eyes ('43)
- ❑ ❑ 2 - The Iron Gates ('45)

Paul Prye
- ❑ ❑ 1 - The Invisible Worm ('41)
- ❑ ❑ 2 - The Weak-Eyed Bat ('42)
- ❑ ❑ 3 - The Devil Loves Me ('42)

Tom Aragon
- ❑ ❑ 1 - Ask Me for Tomorrow ('76)
- ❑ ❑ 2 - The Murder of Miranda ('79)
- ❑ ❑ 3 - Mermaid ('82)

MILLHISER, Marlys
Charlie Greene
- ❑ ❑ 1 - Murder at Moot Point ('92)
- ❑ ❑ 2 - Death of the Office Witch ('93)
- ❑ ❑ 3 - Murder in a Hot Flash ('95)

MITCHELL, Gladys
Beatrice Lestrange Bradley
- ❑ ❑ 1 - Speedy Death ('29)
- ❑ ❑ 2 - The Mystery of a Butcher's Shop ('29)
- ❑ ❑ 3 - The Longer Bodies ('30)
- ❑ ❑ 4 - The Saltmarsh Murders ('32)
- ❑ ❑ 5 - Death at the Opera ('34)
  [Britain-Death in the Wet]
- ❑ ❑ 6 - The Devil at Saxon Wall ('35)
- ❑ ❑ 7 - Dead Men's Morris ('36)
- ❑ ❑ 8 - Come Away, Death ('37)
- ❑ ❑ 9 - St. Peter's Finger ('38)
- ❑ ❑ 10 - Printer's Error ('39)
- ❑ ❑ 11 - Brazen Tongue ('40)
- ❑ ❑ 12 - When Last I Died ('41)
- ❑ ❑ 13 - Hangman's Curfew ('41)
- ❑ ❑ 14 - Laurels are Poison ('42)
- ❑ ❑ 15 - The Worsted Viper ('43)
- ❑ ❑ 16 - Sunset Over Soho ('43)
- ❑ ❑ 17 - The Rising of the Moon ('45)
- ❑ ❑ 18 - Here Comes a Chopper ('46)

❏ ❏ 65 - The Crozier Pharaohs ('84)
❏ ❏ 66 - No Winding-Sheet ('84)

MITCHELL, Kay
John Morrissey
❏ ❏ 1 - A Lively Form of Death ('90)
❏ ❏ 2 - In Stony Places ('91)
❏ ❏ 3 - A Strange Desire ('94) [U.S.–Roots of Evil]

MOFFAT, Gwen
Melinda Pink
❏ ❏ 1 - Lady with a Cool Eye ('73)
❏ ❏ 2 - Miss Pink at the Edge of the World ('75)
❏ ❏ 3 - Over the Sea to Death ('76)
❏ ❏ 4 - A Short Time to Live ('76)
❏ ❏ 5 - Persons Unknown ('78)
❏ ❏ 6 - The Buckskin Girl ('82)
❏ ❏ 7 - Miss Pink's Mistake ('82)
❏ ❏ 8 - Die Like a Dog ('82)
❏ ❏ 9 - Last Chance Country ('83)
❏ ❏ 10 - Grizzly Trail ('84)
❏ ❏ 11 - Snare ('87)
❏ ❏ 12 - The Stone Hawk ('89)
❏ ❏ 13 - Rage ('90)
❏ ❏ 14 - Veronica's Sisters ('92)

MONFREDO, Miriam Grace
Glynis Tryon
❏ ❏ 1 - Seneca Falls Inheritance ('92) ☆ ☆
❏ ❏ 2 - North Star Conspiracy ('93)
❏ ❏ 3 - Blackwater Spirits ('95)
❏ ❏ 4 - Through a Gold Eagle ('96)

MONTGOMERY, Yvonne E.
Finny Aletter
❏ ❏ 1 - Scavengers ('87)
❏ ❏ 2 - Obstacle Course ('90)

MOODY, Susan
Cassandra Swann
❏ ❏ 1 - Death Takes a Hand ('93)
        [Britain-Takeout Double]
❏ ❏ 2 - Grand Slam ('94)
❏ ❏ 3 - King of Hearts ('95)
Penny Wanawake
❏ ❏ 1 - Penny Black ('84)

❑ ❑ 2 - Penny Dreadful ('84)
❑ ❑ 3 - Penny Post ('85)
❑ ❑ 4 - Penny Royal ('86)
❑ ❑ 5 - Penny Wise ('88)
❑ ❑ 6 - Penny Pinching ('89)
❑ ❑ 7 - Penny Saving ('93)

MOORE, Barbara
Dr. Gordon Christy
❑ ❑ 1 - The Doberman Wore Black ('83)
❑ ❑ 2 - The Wolf Whispered Death ('86)

MORGAN, Kate 🄿
Dewey James
❑ ❑ 1 - A Slay at the Races ('90)
❑ ❑ 2 - Murder Most Fowl ('91)
❑ ❑ 3 - Home Sweet Homicide ('92)
❑ ❑ 4 - Mystery Loves Company ('92)
❑ ❑ 5 - Days of Crime and Roses ('92)
❑ ❑ 6 - Wanted Dude or Alive ('94)

MORICE, Anne 🄿
Tessa Crichton
❑ ❑ 1 - Death in the Grand Manor ('70)
❑ ❑ 2 - Murder in Married Life ('71)
❑ ❑ 3 - Death of a Gay Dog ('73)
❑ ❑ 4 - Murder on French Leave ('73)
❑ ❑ 5 - Death and the Dutiful Daughter ('74)
❑ ❑ 6 - Death of a Heavenly Twin ('74)
❑ ❑ 7 - Killing with Kindness ('75)
❑ ❑ 8 - Nursery Tea and Poison ('75)
❑ ❑ 9 - Death of a Wedding Guest ('76)
❑ ❑ 10 - Murder in Mimicry ('77)
❑ ❑ 11 - Scared to Death ('77)
❑ ❑ 12 - Murder by Proxy ('78)
❑ ❑ 13 - Murder in Outline ('79)
❑ ❑ 14 - Death in the Round ('70)
❑ ❑ 15 - The Men in Her Death ('81)
❑ ❑ 16 - Sleep of Death ('82)
❑ ❑ 17 - Hollow Vengeance ('82)
❑ ❑ 18 - Murder Post-Dated ('83)
❑ ❑ 19 - Getting Away with Murder ('84)
❑ ❑ 20 - Dead on Cue ('85)
❑ ❑ 21 - Publish and Be Killed ('86)
❑ ❑ 22 - Treble Exposure ('87)
❑ ❑ 23 - Fatal Charm ('88)

MORISON, B. J.
Elizabeth Lamb Worthington
- ❏ ❏ 1 - Champagne and a Gardener ('82)
- ❏ ❏ 2 - Port and a Star Border ('84)
- ❏ ❏ 3 - Beer and Skittles ('85)
- ❏ ❏ 4 - The Voyage of the Chianti ('87)
- ❏ ❏ 5 - The Martini Effect ('92)

MORRELL, Mary
Lucia Ramos
- ❏ ❏ 1 - Final Session ('91)
- ❏ ❏ 2 - Final Rest ('93)

MOYES, Patricia
Henry & Emmy Tibbett
- ❏ ❏ 1 - Dead Men Don't Ski ('59)
- ❏ ❏ 2 - Down Among the Dead Men ('61)
- ❏ ❏ 3 - Death on the Agenda ('62)
- ❏ ❏ 4 - Murder a la Mode ('63)
- ❏ ❏ 5 - Falling Star ('64)
- ❏ ❏ 6 - Johnny Underground ('65)
- ❏ ❏ 7 - Murder Fantastical ('67)
- ❏ ❏ 8 - Death and the Dutch Uncle ('68)
- ❏ ❏ 9 - Many Deadly Returns ('70) ☆
- ❏ ❏ 10 - Season of Snows and Sins ('71) ★
- ❏ ❏ 11 - The Curious Affair of the Third Dog ('73)
- ❏ ❏ 12 - Black Widower ('75)
- ❏ ❏ 13 - The Coconut Killings ('77)
- ❏ ❏ 14 - Who Is Simon Warwick? ('79)
- ❏ ❏ 15 - Angel Death ('80)
- ❏ ❏ 16 - A Six-Letter Word for Death ('83)
- ❏ ❏ 17 - Night Ferry to Death ('85)
- ❏ ❏ 18 - Black Girl, White Girl ('89)
- ❏ ❏ 19 - Twice in a Blue Moon ('93)

MULLER, Marcia
Elena Oliverez
- ❏ ❏ 1 - The Tree of Death ('83)
- ❏ ❏ 2 - The Legend of the Slain Soldiers ('85)
- ❏ ❏ 3 - Beyond the Grave ('86) [with Bill Pronzini]
Joanna Stark
- ❏ ❏ 1 - The Cavalier in White ('86)
- ❏ ❏ 2 - There Hangs the Knife ('88)
- ❏ ❏ 3 - Dark Star ('89)

Sharon McCone
- ❏ ❏ 1 - Edwin of the Iron Shoes ('77)
- ❏ ❏ 2 - Ask the Cards a Question ('82)
- ❏ ❏ 3 - The Cheshire Cat's Eye ('83)
- ❏ ❏ 4 - Games to Keep the Dark Away ('84)
- ❏ ❏ 5 - Leave a Message for Willie ('84)
- ❏ ❏ 6 - Double [with Bill Pronzini] ('84)
- ❏ ❏ 7 - There's Nothing To Be Afraid Of ('85)
- ❏ ❏ 8 - Eye of the Storm ('88)
- ❏ ❏ 9 - There's Something in a Sunday ('89)
- ❏ ❏ 10 - The Shape of Dread ('89) ★ ☆
- ❏ ❏ 11 - Trophies and Dead Things ('90)
- ❏ ❏ 12 - Where Echoes Live ('91) ☆
- ❏ ❏ 13 - Pennies on a Dead Woman's Eyes ('92)
- ❏ ❏ 14 - Wolf in the Shadows ('93) ★ ☆ ☆
- ❏ ❏ 15 - Till the Butchers Cut Him Down ('94)
- ❏ ❏ 16 - The McCone Files [15 short stories] ('95)
- ❏ ❏ 17 - A Wild and Lonely Place ('95)

MURRAY, Donna Huston
Ginger Struve Barnes
- ❏ ❏ 1 - The Main Line Is Murder ('95)
- ❏ ❏ 2 - Final Arrangements ('96)

MYERS, Amy
Auguste Didier
- ❏ ❏ 1 - Murder in Pug's Parlour ('82)
- ❏ ❏ 2 - Murder in the Limelight ('87)
- ❏ ❏ 3 - Murder at Plum's ('89)
- ❏ ❏ 4 - Murder at the Masque ('91)
- ❏ ❏ 5 - Murder Makes an Entree ('92)
- ❏ ❏ 6 - Murder Under the Kissing Bough ('92)
- ❏ ❏ 7 - Murder in the Smokehouse ('94)

MYERS, Tamar
Magdalena Yoder
- ❏ ❏ 1 - Too Many Crooks Spoil the Broth ('94)
- ❏ ❏ 2 - Parsley, Sage, Rosemary and Crime ('95)

Can you name the award-winning private eye writer who holds an MBA and PhD from the University of Chicago? She was once a marketing manager for a major insurance company.

n

NABB, Magdalen
Salvatore Guarnaccia
- ❏ ❏ 1 - Death of an Englishman ('81)
- ❏ ❏ 2 - Death of a Dutchman ('82)
- ❏ ❏ 3 - Death in Springtime ('83)
- ❏ ❏ 4 - Death in Autumn ('84)
- ❏ ❏ 5 - The Marshal and the Murderer ('87)
- ❏ ❏ 6 - The Marshal and the Madwoman ('88)
- ❏ ❏ 7 - The Marshal's Own Case ('90)
- ❏ ❏ 8 - The Marshal Makes His Report ('91)
- ❏ ❏ 9 - The Marshal at the Villa Torrini ('94)

NEEL, Janet P
John McLeish & Francesca Wilson
- ❏ ❏ 1 - Death's Bright Angel ('88) ★
- ❏ ❏ 2 - Death on Site ('89)
- ❏ ❏ 3 - Death of a Partner ('91)
- ❏ ❏ 4 - Death Among the Dons ('93)

NEELY, Barbara
Blanche White
- ❏ ❏ 1 - Blanche on the Lam ('92) ★ ★ ★
- ❏ ❏ 2 - Blanche Among the Talented Tenth ('94)

NEWMAN, Sharan
Catherine LeVendeur
- ❏ ❏ 1 - Death Comes as Epiphany ('93) ☆ ☆ ☆
- ❏ ❏ 2 - The Devil's Door ('94)
- ❏ ❏ 3 - The Wandering Arm ('95)

NIELSEN, Helen
Simon Drake
- ❏ ❏ 1 - Gold Coast Nocturne ('51)
  [Britain-Murder by Proxy]
- ❏ ❏ 2 - After Midnight ('66)
- ❏ ❏ 3 - A Killer in the Street ('67)
- ❏ ❏ 4 - Darkest Hour ('69)
- ❏ ❏ 5 - The Severed Key ('73)
- ❏ ❏ 6 - The Brink of Murder ('76)

NORTH, Suzanne
Phoebe Fairfax
- ❏ ❏ 1 - Healthy, Wealthy & Dead ('94) ☆

☰☰☰☰☰☰☰☰☰☰ *O* ☰☰☰☰☰☰☰☰☰☰

O'BRIEN, Meg
Jessica James
- ❑ ❑ 1 - The Daphne Decisions ('90)
- ❑ ❑ 2 - Salmon in the Soup ('90)
- ❑ ❑ 3 - Hare Today, Gone Tomorrow ('91)
- ❑ ❑ 4 - Eagles Die Too ('92)
- ❑ ❑ 5 - Thin Ice ('93)

O'CALLAGHAN, Maxine
Dr. Anne Menlo
- ❑ ❑ 1 - Shadow of a Child ('96)
- ❑ ❑ 2 - Ashes to Ashes ('97)
Delilah West
- ❑ ❑ 1 - Death Is Forever ('80)
- ❑ ❑ 2 - Run from Nightmare ('81)
- ❑ ❑ 3 - Hit and Run ('89)
- ❑ ❑ 4 - Set-Up ('91)
- ❑ ❑ 5 - Trade-Off ('94)

O'CONNELL, Carol
Kathleen Mallory
- ❑ ❑ 1 - Mallory's Oracle ('94) ☆ ☆
- ❑ ❑ 2 - The Man Who Cast Two Shadows ('95)

O'CONNELL, Catherine
Karen Levinson
- ❑ ❑ 1 - Skins ('93)

O'DONNELL, Lillian
Gwenn Ramadge
- ❑ ❑ 1 - A Wreath for the Bride ('90)
- ❑ ❑ 2 - Used to Kill ('93)
- ❑ ❑ 3 - Raggedy Man ('95)
Mici Anhalt
- ❑ ❑ 1 - Aftershock ('77)
- ❑ ❑ 2 - Falling Star ('79)
- ❑ ❑ 3 - Wicked Designs ('80)
Norah Mulcahaney
- ❑ ❑ 1 - The Phone Calls ('72)
- ❑ ❑ 2 - Don't Wear Your Wedding Ring ('73)
- ❑ ❑ 3 - Dial 557 R-A-P-E ('74)
- ❑ ❑ 4 - The Baby Merchants ('75)
- ❑ ❑ 5 - Leisure Dying ('76)

❏ ❏ 6 - No Business Being a Cop ('79)
❏ ❏ 7 - The Children's Zoo ('81)
❏ ❏ 8 - Cop Without a Shield ('83)
❏ ❏ 9 - Ladykiller ('84)
❏ ❏ 10 - Casual Affairs ('85)
❏ ❏ 11 - The Other Side of the Door ('87)
❏ ❏ 12 - A Good Night to Kill ('89) ★
❏ ❏ 13 - A Private Crime ('91)
❏ ❏ 14 - Pushover ('92)
❏ ❏ 15 - Lockout ('94)

O'MARIE, Sister Carol Anne
Sister Mary Helen
❏ ❏ 1 - A Novena for Murder ('84)
❏ ❏ 2 - Advent of Dying ('86)
❏ ❏ 3 - The Missing Madonna ('88)
❏ ❏ 4 - Murder in Ordinary Time ('91)
❏ ❏ 5 - Murder Makes a Pilgrimmage ('93)
❏ ❏ 6 - Death Goes on Retreat ('95)

OCORK, Shannon
Theresa Tracy Baldwin
❏ ❏ 1 - Sports Freak ('80)
❏ ❏ 2 - End of the Line ('81)
❏ ❏ 3 - Hell Bent for Heaven ('83)

OFFORD, Lenore Glen
Bill & Coco Hastings
❏ ❏ 1 - Murder on Russian Hill ('38)
          [Britain-Murder Before Breakfast]
❏ ❏ 2 - Clues to Burn ('42)
Todd McKinnon & Georgine Wyeth
❏ ❏ 1 - Skeleton Key ('43)
❏ ❏ 2 - The Glass Mask ('44)
❏ ❏ 3 - The Smiling Tiger ('49)
❏ ❏ 4 - Walking Shadow ('59)

OLEKSIW, Susan
Joe Silva
❏ ❏ 1 - Murder in Mellingham ('93)
❏ ❏ 2 - Double Take ('94)
❏ ❏ 3 - Family Album ('95)

 Can you name two mystery series set in national parks featuring park ranger sleuths?

OLIPHANT, B. J. ▣
Shirley McClintock
- ❏ ❏ 1 - Dead in the Scrub ('90) ☆
- ❏ ❏ 2 - The Unexpected Corpse ('90)
- ❏ ❏ 3 - Deservedly Dead ('92)
- ❏ ❏ 4 - Death and the Delinquent ('92)
- ❏ ❏ 5 - Death Served Up Cold ('94)

OLIVER, Maria Antonia
Lonia Gulu
- ❏ ❏ 1 - A Study in Lilac ('87)
- ❏ ❏ 2 - Antipodes ('89)

OLSEN, D. B. ▣
Prof. A. Pennyfather
- ❏ ❏ 1 - Bring the Bride a Shroud ('45)
  [APA–A Shroud for the Bride]
- ❏ ❏ 2 - Gallows for the Groom ('47)
- ❏ ❏ 3 - Devious Design ('48)
- ❏ ❏ 4 - Something About Midnight ('50)
- ❏ ❏ 5 - Love Me in Death ('51)
- ❏ ❏ 6 - Enrollment Cancelled ('52)
  [APA–Dead Babes in the Wood]

Rachel & Jennifer Murdock
- ❏ ❏ 1 - The Cat Saw Murder ('39)
- ❏ ❏ 2 - The Alarm of the Black Cat ('42)
- ❏ ❏ 3 - Cat's Claw ('43)
- ❏ ❏ 4 - Catspaw for Murder ('43)
- ❏ ❏ 5 - The Cat Wears a Noose ('44)
- ❏ ❏ 6 - Cats Don't Smile ('45)
- ❏ ❏ 7 - Cats Don't Need Coffins ('46)
- ❏ ❏ 8 - Cats Have Tall Shadows ('48)
- ❏ ❏ 9 - The Cat Wears a Mask ('49)
- ❏ ❏ 10 - Death Wears Cat's Eyes ('50)
- ❏ ❏ 11 - The Cat and Capricorn ('51)
- ❏ ❏ 12 - The Cat Walk ('53)
- ❏ ❏ 13 - Death Walks on Cat Feet ('56)

Lt. Stephen Mayhew
- ❏ ❏ 1 - The Ticking Heart ('40)
- ❏ ❏ 2 - The Clue in the Clay ('48)

What mystery writer developed an advertising campaign featuring the British cartoon that inspired the creation of Col. Mustard?

ORDE, A. J. 🄿
Jason Lynx
- ❏ ❏ 1 - A Little Neighborhood Murder ('89)
- ❏ ❏ 2 - Death and the Dogwalker ('90)
- ❏ ❏ 3 - Death for Old Times' Sake ('92)
- ❏ ❏ 4 - Looking for the Aardvark ('93)
  [APA–Dead on Sunday]
- ❏ ❏ 5 - A Long Time Dead ('95)

OSBORNE, Denise
Queenie Davilow
- ❏ ❏ 1 - Murder Offscreen ('94)
- ❏ ❏ 2 - Cut to: Murder ('95)

𝒫

PADGETT, Abigail
Barbara Joan "Bo" Bradley
- ❏ ❏ 1 - Child of Silence ('93) ☆ ☆
- ❏ ❏ 2 - Strawgirl ('94)
- ❏ ❏ 3 - Turtle Baby ('95)

PAGE, Emma 🄿
Insp. Kelsey
- ❏ ❏ 1 - Missing Woman ('80)
- ❏ ❏ 2 - Every Second Thursday ('81)
- ❏ ❏ 3 - Last Walk Home ('82)
- ❏ ❏ 4 - Cold Light of Day ('83)
- ❏ ❏ 5 - Scent of Death ('85)
- ❏ ❏ 6 - Final Moments ('87)
- ❏ ❏ 7 - A Violent End ('88)

PAGE, Katherine Hall
Faith Sibley Fairchild
- ❏ ❏ 1 - The Body in the Belfry ('90) ★
- ❏ ❏ 2 - The Body in the Kelp ('91)
- ❏ ❏ 3 - The Body in the Bouillon ('91)
- ❏ ❏ 4 - The Body in the Vestibule ('92)
- ❏ ❏ 5 - The Body in the Cast ('93)
- ❏ ❏ 6 - The Body in the Basement ('94)
- ❏ ❏ 7 - The Body in the Bog ('96)

PAIGE, Robin 🄿
Kathryn Ardleigh
- ❏ ❏ 1 - Death at Bishop's Keep ('94)
- ❏ ❏ 2 - Death at Gallows Green ('95)

PAPAZOGLOU, Orania

Patience Campbell McKenna

- ❑ ❑ 1 - Sweet, Savage Death ('84) ☆
- ❑ ❑ 2 - Wicked, Loving Murder ('85)
- ❑ ❑ 3 - Death's Savage Passion ('86)
- ❑ ❑ 4 - Rich, Radiant Slaughter ('88)
- ❑ ❑ 5 - Once and Always Murder ('90)

PARETSKY, Sara

V. I. Warshawski

- ❑ ❑ 1 - Indemnity Only ('82)
- ❑ ❑ 2 - Deadlock ('84)
- ❑ ❑ 3 - Killing Orders ('85)
- ❑ ❑ 4 - Bitter Medicine ('87)
- ❑ ❑ 5 - Blood Shot ('88) ★ ☆ ☆
  [Britain-Toxic Shock]
- ❑ ❑ 6 - Burn Marks ('90)
- ❑ ❑ 7 - Guardian Angel ('91)
- ❑ ❑ 8 - Tunnel Vision ('94)
- ❑ ❑ 9 - Windy City Blues [short stories] ('95)

PARKER, Barbara

Gail Connor

- ❑ ❑ 1 - Suspicion of Innocence ('94) ☆
- ❑ ❑ 2 - Suspicion of Guilt ('95)

PAUL, Barbara

Enrico Caruso

- ❑ ❑ 1 - A Cadenza for Caruso ('84)
- ❑ ❑ 2 - Prima Donna at Large ('85)
- ❑ ❑ 3 - A Chorus of Detectives ('87)

Marian Larch

- ❑ ❑ 1 - The Renewable Virgin ('84)
- ❑ ❑ 2 - You Have the Right to Remain Silent ('92)
- ❑ ❑ 3 - The Apostrophe Thief ('93)
- ❑ ❑ 4 - Fare Play ('95)

PENCE, Joanne

Angelina Amalfi

- ❑ ❑ 1 - Something's Cooking ('93)
- ❑ ❑ 2 - Too Many Cooks ('94)
- ❑ ❑ 3 - Cooking Up Trouble ('95)

PERRY, Anne

Thomas & Charlotte Pitt

- ❑ ❑ 1 - The Cater Street Hangman ('79)
- ❑ ❑ 2 - Callander Square ('80)
- ❑ ❑ 3 - Paragon Walk ('81)
- ❑ ❑ 4 - Resurrection Row ('81)
- ❑ ❑ 5 - Rutland Place ('83)
- ❑ ❑ 6 - Bluegate Fields ('84)
- ❑ ❑ 7 - Death in Devil's Acre ('85)
- ❑ ❑ 8 - Cardington Crescent ('87)
- ❑ ❑ 9 - Silence in Hanover Close ('88)
- ❑ ❑ 10 - Bethlehem Road ('90)
- ❑ ❑ 11 - Highgate Rise ('91)
- ❑ ❑ 12 - Belgrave Square ('92)
- ❑ ❑ 13 - Farrier's Lane ('93)
- ❑ ❑ 14 - The Hyde Park Headsman ('94)
- ❑ ❑ 15 - Traitor's Gate ('95)

William Monk

- ❑ ❑ 1 - The Face of a Stranger ('90) ☆
- ❑ ❑ 2 - A Dangerous Mourning ('91)
- ❑ ❑ 3 - Defend and Betray ('92) ★ ☆
- ❑ ❑ 4 - A Sudden, Fearful Death ('93)
- ❑ ❑ 5 - Sins of the Wolf ('94)
- ❑ ❑ 6 - Cain His Brother ('95)

PETERS, Elizabeth ℙ

Amelia Peabody

- ❑ ❑ 1 - Crocodile on the Sandbank ('75)
- ❑ ❑ 2 - The Curse of the Pharaohs ('81)
- ❑ ❑ 3 - The Mummy Case ('85)
- ❑ ❑ 4 - Lion in the Valley ('86)
- ❑ ❑ 5 - The Deeds of the Disturber ('88)
- ❑ ❑ 6 - The Last Camel Died at Noon ('91) ☆
- ❑ ❑ 7 - The Snake, the Crocodile and the Dog ('92) ☆

Jacqueline Kirby

- ❑ ❑ 1 - The Seventh Sinner ('72)
- ❑ ❑ 2 - The Murders of Richard III ('74)
- ❑ ❑ 3 - Die for Love ('84)
- ❑ ❑ 4 - Naked Once More ('89) ★ ★

Who stars in the longest-running police series (1960–1987) ever written by an American woman? With over 60 police novels, she was "Queen of the procedurals."

Vicky Bliss

- ❏ ❏ 1 - Borrower of the Night ('73)
- ❏ ❏ 2 - Street of the Five Moons ('78)
- ❏ ❏ 3 - Silhouette in Scarlet ('83)
- ❏ ❏ 4 - Trojan Gold ('87)
- ❏ ❏ 5 - Night Train to Memphis ('94) ☆

PETERS, Ellis 🅟

Brother Cadfael

- ❏ ❏ 1 - A Morbid Taste for Bones ('77)
- ❏ ❏ 2 - One Corpse Too Many ('79)
- ❏ ❏ 3 - Monk's Hood ('80) ★
- ❏ ❏ 4 - St. Peter's Fair ('81)
- ❏ ❏ 5 - The Leper of St. Giles ('81)
- ❏ ❏ 6 - The Virgin in the Ice ('82)
- ❏ ❏ 7 - The Sanctuary Sparrow ('83)
- ❏ ❏ 8 - The Devil's Novice ('83)
- ❏ ❏ 9 - The Dead Man's Ransom ('84)
- ❏ ❏ 10 - The Pilgrim of Hate ('84)
- ❏ ❏ 11 - An Excellent Mystery ('85)
- ❏ ❏ 12 - The Raven in the Foregate ('86)
- ❏ ❏ 13 - The Rose Rent ('86)
- ❏ ❏ 14 - The Hermit of Eyton Forest ('87)
- ❏ ❏ 15 - The Confession of Brother Haluin ('88)
- ❏ ❏ 16 - The Heretic's Apprentice ('89)
- ❏ ❏ 17 - The Potter's Field ('89) ☆
- ❏ ❏ 18 - Summer of the Danes ('91)
- ❏ ❏ 19 - The Holy Thief ('92)
- ❏ ❏ 20 - Brother Cadfael's Penance ('94)

George, Bunty & Dominic Felse

- ❏ ❏ 1 - Fallen into the Pit ('51)
- ❏ ❏ 2 - Death and the Joyful Woman ('62) ★
- ❏ ❏ 3 - Flight of a Witch ('64)
- ❏ ❏ 4 - A Nice Derangement of Epitaphs ('65)
      [U.S.-Who Lies Here]
- ❏ ❏ 5 - The Piper on the Mountain ('66)
- ❏ ❏ 6 - Black Is the Colour of My True Love's Heart ('67)
- ❏ ❏ 7 - The Grass Widow's Tale ('68)
- ❏ ❏ 8 - The House of Green Turf ('69)
- ❏ ❏ 9 - Morning Raga ('69)
- ❏ ❏ 10 - The Knocker on Death's Door (70)
- ❏ ❏ 11 - Death to the Landlords! ('72)
- ❏ ❏ 12 - City of Gold and Shadows ('73)
- ❏ ❏ 13 - Rainbow's End ('78)

PETERSON, Audrey Ⓟ
Claire Camden
❑ ❑ 1 - Dartmoor Burial ('92)
❑ ❑ 2 - Death Too Soon ('94)
❑ ❑ 3 - Shroud for a Scholar ('95)
Jane Winfield
❑ ❑ 1 - The Nocturne Murder ('88)
❑ ❑ 2 - Death in Wessex ('89)
❑ ❑ 3 - Murder in Burgundy ('89)
❑ ❑ 4 - Deadly Rehearsal ('90)
❑ ❑ 5 - Elegy in a Country Graveyard ('90)
❑ ❑ 6 - Lament for Christabel ('91)

PETRIE, Rhona Ⓟ
Marcus MacLurg
❑ ❑ 1 - Death in Deakins Wood ('63)
❑ ❑ 2 - Murder by Precedent ('64)
❑ ❑ 3 - Running Deep ('65)
❑ ❑ 4 - Dead Loss ('66)
❑ ❑ 5 - MacLurg Goes West ('68)

PICKARD, Nancy
Jenny Cain
❑ ❑ 1 - Generous Death ('84)
❑ ❑ 2 - Say No to Murder ('85) ★
❑ ❑ 3 - No Body ('86) ☆
❑ ❑ 4 - Marriage Is Murder ('87) ★ ☆
❑ ❑ 5 - Dead Crazy ('88) ☆ ☆
❑ ❑ 6 - Bum Steer ('89) ★
❑ ❑ 7 - I. O. U. ('91) ★ ★ ☆
❑ ❑ 8 - But I Wouldn't Want to Die There ('93)
❑ ❑ 9 - Confession ('94)
❑ ❑ 10 - Twilight ('95)

PIESMAN, Marissa
Nina Fischman
❑ ❑ 1 - Unorthodox Practices ('89)
❑ ❑ 2 - Personal Effects ('91)
❑ ❑ 3 - Heading Uptown ('93)
❑ ❑ 4 - Close Quarters ('94)
❑ ❑ 5 - Alternate Sides ('95)

What daughter of a former United States president has her own mystery series set in Washington D.C.?

PINCUS, Elizabeth

Nell Fury

- ❑ ❑ 1 - The Two-Bit Tango ('92)
- ❑ ❑ 2 - The Solitary Twist ('93)
- ❑ ❑ 3 - The Hangdog Hustle ('95)

POPKIN, Zelda

Mary Carner

- ❑ ❑ 1 - Death Wears a White Gardenia ('38)
- ❑ ❑ 2 - Murder in the Mist ('40)
- ❑ ❑ 3 - Time Off for Murder ('40)
- ❑ ❑ 4 - Dead Man's Gift ('41)
- ❑ ❑ 5 - No Crime for a Lady ('42)

PORATH, Sharon

Kendra MacFarlane

- ❑ ❑ 1 - Dead File ('95)

PORTER, Anna

Judith Hayes

- ❑ ❑ 1 - Hidden Agenda ('85)
- ❑ ❑ 2 - Mortal Sins ('87)

PORTER, Joyce

Honorable Constance Ethel Morrison Burke

- ❑ ❑ 1 - Rather a Common Sort of Crime ('70)
- ❑ ❑ 2 - A Meddler and Her Murder ('72)
- ❑ ❑ 3 - The Package Included Murder ('75)
- ❑ ❑ 4 - Who the Heck Is Sylvia? ('77)
- ❑ ❑ 5 - The Cart Before the Crime ('79)

Eddie Brown

- ❑ ❑ 1 - Sour Cream with Everything ('66)
- ❑ ❑ 2 - The Chinks in the Curtain ('67)
- ❑ ❑ 3 - Neither a Candle nor a Pitchfork ('69)
- ❑ ❑ 4 - Only with a Bargepole ('71)

Wilfred Dover

- ❑ ❑ 1 - Dover One ('64)
- ❑ ❑ 2 - Dover Two ('65)
- ❑ ❑ 3 - Dover Three ('65)
- ❑ ❑ 4 - Dover and the Unkindest Cut of All ('67)
- ❑ ❑ 5 - Dover and the Sense of Justice ('68)
- ❑ ❑ 6 - Dover Goes to Pott ('68)
- ❑ ❑ 7 - Dover Pulls a Rabbit ('69)
- ❑ ❑ 8 - Dover Fails to Make His Mark ('70)
- ❑ ❑ 9 - Dover Strikes Again ('70)

❑ ❑ 10 - A Terrible Drag for Dover ('71)
❑ ❑ 11 - Dover and the Dark Lady ('72)
❑ ❑ 12 - It's Murder with Dover ('73)
❑ ❑ 13 - Dover Tangles with High Finance ('75)
❑ ❑ 14 - Dover and the Claret Tappers ('76)
❑ ❑ 15 - Dover Does Some Spadework ('77)
❑ ❑ 16 - When Dover Gets Knotted ('77)
❑ ❑ 17 - Dover Without Perks ('78)
❑ ❑ 18 - Dover Doesn't Dilly-Dally ('78)
❑ ❑ 19 - Dead Easy for Dover ('78)
❑ ❑ 20 - Dover Goes to School ('78)
❑ ❑ 21 - Dover Beats the Band ('80)

POWELL, Deborah
Hollis Carpenter
❑ ❑ 1 - Bayou City Streets ('91)
❑ ❑ 2 - Houston Town ('92)

PROWELL, Sandra West
Phoebe Siegel
❑ ❑ 1 - By Evil Means ('93) ☆
❑ ❑ 2 - The Killing of Monday Brown ('94) ☆
❑ ❑ 3 - Death of a Wallflower ('95)

PUGH, Dianne G.
Iris Thorne
❑ ❑ 1 - Cold Call ('93)
❑ ❑ 2 - Slow Squeeze ('94)

PULVER, Mary Monica
Peter & Kori Price Brichter
❑ ❑ 1 - Murder at the War ('87)
[APA–Knight Fall]
❑ ❑ 2 - The Unforgiving Minutes [prequel] ('88)
❑ ❑ 3 - Ashes to Ashes ('88)
❑ ❑ 4 - Original Sin ('91)
❑ ❑ 5 - Show Stopper ('92)

Q

QUEST, Erica ▣
Kate Maddox
❑ ❑ 1 - Death Walk ('88)
❑ ❑ 2 - Cold Coffin ('90)

QUINN, Elizabeth
Lauren Maxwell
- ❑ ❑ 1 - Murder Most Grizzly ('93)
- ❑ ❑ 2 - A Wolf in Death's Clothing ('95)

RADLEY, Sheila ▣
Douglas Quantrill & Hilary Lloyd
- ❑ ❑ 1 - Death and the Maiden ('78)
  [U.S.-Death in the Morning]
- ❑ ❑ 2 - The Chief Inspector's Daughter ('80)
- ❑ ❑ 3 - A Talent for Destruction ('82)
- ❑ ❑ 4 - Blood on the Happy Highway ('83)
  [U.S.-The Quiet Road to Death]
- ❑ ❑ 5 - Fate Worse Than Death ('85)
- ❑ ❑ 6 - Who Saw Him Die? ('87)
- ❑ ❑ 7 - This Way Out ('89)
- ❑ ❑ 8 - Cross My Heart and Hope to Die ('92)
- ❑ ❑ 9 - Fair Game ('94)

REDMANN, J. M.
Michelle "Micky" Knight
- ❑ ❑ 1 - Death by the Riverside ('90)
- ❑ ❑ 2 - Deaths of Jocasta ('93) ☆
- ❑ ❑ 3 - The Intersection of Law and Desire ('95)

REILLY, Helen
Christopher McKee
- ❑ ❑ 1 - The Diamond Feather ('30)
- ❑ ❑ 2 - Murder in the Mews ('31)
- ❑ ❑ 3 - McKee of Centre Street ('34)
- ❑ ❑ 4 - The Line-up ('34)
- ❑ ❑ 5 - Mr. Smith's Hat ('36)
- ❑ ❑ 6 - Dead Man's Control ('36)
- ❑ ❑ 7 - Dead for a Ducat ('39)
- ❑ ❑ 8 - All Concerned Notified ('39)
- ❑ ❑ 9 - Murder in Shinbone Alley ('40)
- ❑ ❑ 10 - Death Demands an Audience ('40)
- ❑ ❑ 11 - The Dead Can Tell ('40)
- ❑ ❑ 12 - Mourned on Sunday ('41)
- ❑ ❑ 13 - Three Women in Black ('41)
- ❑ ❑ 14 - Name Your Poison ('42)
- ❑ ❑ 15 - The Opening Door ('44)
- ❑ ❑ 16 - Murder on Angler's Island ('45)

- ❑ ❑ 17 - The Silver Leopard ('46)
- ❑ ❑ 18 - The Farmhouse ('47)
- ❑ ❑ 19 - Staircase 4 ('49)
- ❑ ❑ 20 - Murder at Arroways ('50)
- ❑ ❑ 21 - Lament for the Bride ('51)
- ❑ ❑ 22 - The Double Man ('52)
- ❑ ❑ 23 - The Velvet Hand ('53)
- ❑ ❑ 24 - Tell Her It's Murder ('54)
- ❑ ❑ 25 - Compartment K ('55)
       [Britain-Murder Rides the Express]
- ❑ ❑ 26 - The Canvas Dagger ('56)
- ❑ ❑ 27 - Ding Dong Bell ('58)
- ❑ ❑ 28 - Not Me, Inspector ('59)
- ❑ ❑ 29 - Follow Me ('60)
- ❑ ❑ 30 - Certain Sleep ('61)
- ❑ ❑ 31 - The Day She Died ('62)

RENDELL, Ruth
Reginald Wexford
- ❑ ❑ 1 - From Doon with Death ('64)
- ❑ ❑ 2 - A Wolf to Slaughter ('67)
- ❑ ❑ 3 - A New Lease on Death ('67)
- ❑ ❑ 4 - The Best Man to Die ('69)
- ❑ ❑ 5 - A Guilty Thing Surprised ('70)
- ❑ ❑ 6 - No More Dying Then ('71)
- ❑ ❑ 7 - Murder Being Once Done ('72)
- ❑ ❑ 8 - Some Lie and Some Die ('73)
- ❑ ❑ 9 - Shake Hands Forever ('75)
- ❑ ❑ 10 - A Sleeping Life ('78) ☆
- ❑ ❑ 11 - Put on by Cunning ('81)
       [U.S.-Death Notes]
- ❑ ❑ 12 - The Speaker of Mandarin ('83)
- ❑ ❑ 13 - An Unkindness of Ravens ('85) ☆
- ❑ ❑ 14 - The Veiled One ('88)
- ❑ ❑ 15 - Kissing the Gunner's Daughter ('93)
- ❑ ❑ 16 - Simisola ('94)

RICE, Craig 🅿
Bingo Riggs & Handsome Kusak
- ❑ ❑ 1 - The Sunday Pigeon Murders ('42)
- ❑ ❑ 2 - The Thursday Turkey Murders ('43)
- ❑ ❑ 3 - The April Robin Murders ('58)
John J. Malone
- ❑ ❑ 1 - 8 Faces at 3 ('39)
- ❑ ❑ 2 - The Corpse Steps Out ('40)
- ❑ ❑ 3 - The Wrong Murder ('40)

❑ ❑ 4 - The Right Murder ('41)
❑ ❑ 5 - Trial by Fury ('41)
❑ ❑ 6 - The Big Midget Murders ('42)
❑ ❑ 7 - Having a Wonderful Crime ('43)
❑ ❑ 8 - The Lucky Stiff ('45)
❑ ❑ 9 - The Fourth Postman ('48)
❑ ❑ 10 - My Kingdom for a Hearse ('57)
❑ ❑ 11 - Knocked for a Loop ('57)
　　　　　[Britain-The Double Frame]
❑ ❑ 12 - The Name Is Malone [short stories] ('58)
❑ ❑ 13 - People vs. Withers and Malone
　　　　　[short stories] ('63)
❑ ❑ 14 - But the Doctor Died ('67)

RICH, Virginia
Eugenia Potter
❑ ❑ 1 - The Cooking School Murders ('82)
❑ ❑ 2 - The Baked Bean Supper Murders ('83)
❑ ❑ 3 - The Nantucket Diet Murders ('85)
❑ ❑ 4 - The 27-Ingredient Chili Con Carne Murders
　　　　　('93) [with Nancy Pickard]

RINEHART, Mary Roberts
Hilda Adams
❑ ❑ 1 - Miss Pinkerton ('32)
❑ ❑ 2 - Haunted Lady ('42)
❑ ❑ 3 - The Wandering Knife ('52)

RIPLEY, Ann
Louise Eldridge
❑ ❑ 1 - Mulch ('94)

ROBB, Candace M.
Owen Archer
❑ ❑ 1 - The Apothecary Rose ('93)
❑ ❑ 2 - The Lady Chapel ('94)
❑ ❑ 3 - The Nun's Tale ('95)

ROBB, J. D. 🅿
Eve Dallas
❑ ❑ 1 - Naked in Death ('95)
❑ ❑ 2 - Glory in Death ('96)

? What amateur sleuth owns Goldilocks' Catering, "Where everything is always just right"?

ROBERTS, Carey
Anne Fitzhugh
- ❑ ❑ 1 - Touch a Cold Door ('89)
- ❑ ❑ 2 - Pray God to Die ('93)

ROBERTS, Gillian 🄿
Amanda Pepper
- ❑ ❑ 1 - Caught Dead in Philadelphia ('87) ★
- ❑ ❑ 2 - Philly Stakes ('89) ☆
- ❑ ❑ 3 - I'd Rather Be in Philadelphia ('91)
- ❑ ❑ 4 - With Friends Like These ('93)
- ❑ ❑ 5 - How I Spent My Summer Vacation ('94)
- ❑ ❑ 6 - In the Dead of Summer ('95)

ROBERTS, Lora
Liz Sullivan
- ❑ ❑ 1 - Murder in a Nice Neighborhood ('94)
- ❑ ❑ 2 - Murder in the Marketplace ('95)

ROBINSON, Lynda S.
Lord Meren
- ❑ ❑ 1 - Murder in the Place of Anubis ('94)
- ❑ ❑ 2 - Murder at the God's Gate ('95)
- ❑ ❑ 3 - Murder at the Feast of Rejoicing ('96)

ROBITAILLE, Julie
Kit Powell
- ❑ ❑ 1 - Jinx ('92)
- ❑ ❑ 2 - Iced ('94)

ROMBERG, Nina
Marian Winchester
- ❑ ❑ 1 - The Spirit Stalker ('89)
- ❑ ❑ 2 - Shadow Walkers ('93)

ROOME, Annette
Christine Martin
- ❑ ❑ 1 - A Real Shot in the Arm ('89) ★
- ❑ ❑ 2 - A Second Shot in the Dark ('90)

ROSS, Kate
Julian Kestrel
- ❑ ❑ 1 - Cut to the Quick ('93)
- ❑ ❑ 2 - A Broken Vessel ('94)
- ❑ ❑ 3 - Whom the Gods Love ('95)

ROTHENBERG, Rebecca
Claire Sharples
- ❏ ❏ 1 - The Bulrush Murders ('91) ☆ ☆
- ❏ ❏ 2 - The Dandelion Murders ('94)
- ❏ ❏ 3 - The Shy Tulip Murders ('95)

ROWE, Jennifer
Verity "Birdie" Birdwood
- ❏ ❏ 1 - Murder by the Book ('89)
- ❏ ❏ 2 - Grim Pickings ('91)
- ❏ ❏ 3 - Death in Store [short stories] ('92)
- ❏ ❏ 4 - The Makeover Murders ('93)
- ❏ ❏ 5 - Stranglehold ('94)

ROWLANDS, Betty
Melissa Craig
- ❏ ❏ 1 - Murder in the Cotswolds ('89)
- ❏ ❏ 2 - A Little Gentle Sleuthing ('90)
- ❏ ❏ 3 - Finishing Touch ('93)
- ❏ ❏ 4 - Over the Edge ('93)
- ❏ ❏ 5 - Exhaustive Inquiries ('94)
- ❏ ❏ 6 - Malice Poetic ('95)

ROZAN, S. J.
Lydia Chin & Bill Smith
- ❏ ❏ 1 - China Trade ('94)
- ❏ ❏ 2 - Concourse ('95)

RURYK, Jean
Catherine Wilde
- ❏ ❏ 1 - Chicken Little Was Right ('94)

━━━━━━━━━━━ *S* ━━━━━━━━━━━

SALE, Medora
John Sanders & Harriet Jeffries
- ❏ ❏ 1 - Murder on the Run ('86) ★
- ❏ ❏ 2 - Murder in Focus ('89)
- ❏ ❏ 3 - Murder in a Good Cause ('90)
- ❏ ❏ 4 - Sleep of the Innocent ('91)
- ❏ ❏ 5 - Pursued by Shadows ('92)
- ❏ ❏ 6 - Short Cut to Santa Fe ('94)

SANDSTROM, Eve K.
Sam & Nicky Titus
- ❏ ❏ 1 - Death Down Home ('90)
- ❏ ❏ 2 - The Devil Down Home ('91)
- ❏ ❏ 3 - The Down Home Heifer Heist ('93)

SAUM, Karen
Brigid Donovan
- ❏ ❏ 1 - Murder Is Relative ('90)
- ❏ ❏ 2 - Murder Is Germane ('92)
- ❏ ❏ 3 - Murder Is Material ('94)

SAWYER, Corinne Holt
Angela Benbow & Caledonia Wingate
- ❏ ❏ 1 - The J. Alfred Prufrock Murders ('88) ☆
- ❏ ❏ 2 - Murder in Gray & White ('89)
- ❏ ❏ 3 - Murder by Owl Light ('92)
- ❏ ❏ 4 - The Peanut Butter Murders ('93)
- ❏ ❏ 5 - Murder Has No Calories ('94)
- ❏ ❏ 6 - Ho-Ho Homicide ('95)

SAYERS, Dorothy L.
Lord Peter Wimsey
- ❏ ❏ 1 - Whose Body? ('23)
- ❏ ❏ 2 - Clouds of Witness ('26)
- ❏ ❏ 3 - Unnatural Death ('27)
  [U.S.-The Dawson Pedigree]
- ❏ ❏ 4 - The Unpleasantness at the Bellona Club ('28)
- ❏ ❏ 5 - Lord Peter Views the Body ('29)
- ❏ ❏ 6 - Strong Poison ('30)
- ❏ ❏ 7 - Five Red Herrings ('31)
  [U.S.-Suspicious Characters]
- ❏ ❏ 8 - Have His Carcase ('32)
- ❏ ❏ 9 - Murder Must Advertise ('33)
- ❏ ❏ 10 - Hangman's Holiday [short stories] ('33)
- ❏ ❏ 11 - The Nine Tailors ('34)
- ❏ ❏ 12 - Gaudy Night ('35)
- ❏ ❏ 13 - Busman's Honeymoon ('37)
- ❏ ❏ 14 - In the Teeth of the Evidence ('39)

SCHENKEL, S. E.
Ray & Kate Frederick
- ❏ ❏ 1 - In Blacker Moments ('94)
- ❏ ❏ 2 - Death Days ('95)

SCHERF, Margaret

Emily & Henry Bryce
- ❏ ❏ 1 - The Gun in Daniel Webster's Bust ('49)
- ❏ ❏ 2 - The Green Plaid Pants ('51)
  [APA-The Corpse with One Shoe]
- ❏ ❏ 3 - Glass on the Stairs ('54)
- ❏ ❏ 4 - The Diplomat and the Gold Piano ('63)
  [Britain-Death and the Diplomat]

Dr. Grace Severance
- ❏ ❏ 1 - The Banker's Bones ('68)
- ❏ ❏ 2 - The Beautiful Birthday Cake ('71)
- ❏ ❏ 3 - To Cache a Millionaire ('72)
- ❏ ❏ 4 - The Beaded Banana ('78)

Lt. Ryan
- ❏ ❏ 1 - The Owl in the Cellar ('45)
- ❏ ❏ 2 - Murder Makes Me Nervous ('48)

Rev. Martin Buell
- ❏ ❏ 1 - Always Murder a Friend ('48)
- ❏ ❏ 2 - Gilbert's Last Toothache ('49)
  [APA-For the Love of Murder]
- ❏ ❏ 3 - The Curious Custard Pie ('50)
  [APA-Divine and Deadly]
- ❏ ❏ 4 - The Elk and the Evidence ('52)
- ❏ ❏ 5 - The Cautious Overshoes ('56)
- ❏ ❏ 6 - The Corpse in the Flannel Nightgown ('65)

SCHIER, Norma

Kay Barth
- ❏ ❏ 1 - Death on the Slopes ('78)
- ❏ ❏ 2 - Murder by the Book ('79)
- ❏ ❏ 3 - Death Goes Skiing ('79)
- ❏ ❏ 4 - Demon at the Opera ('80)

SCHMIDT, Carol

Laney Samms
- ❏ ❏ 1 - Silverlake Heat ('93)
- ❏ ❏ 2 - Sweet Cherry Wine ('94)
- ❏ ❏ 3 - Cabin Fever ('94)

SCOPPETTONE, Sandra

Lauren Laurano
- ❏ ❏ 1 - Everything You Have Is Mine ('91)
- ❏ ❏ 2 - I'll Be Leaving You Always ('93)
- ❏ ❏ 3 - My Sweet Untraceable You ('94)

SCOTT, Rosie
Glory Day
❑ ❑ 1 - Glory Day ('89)

SCOTTOLINE, Lisa
Grace Rossi
❑ ❑ 1 - Final Appeal ('94) ★
Mary DiNunzio
❑ ❑ 1 - Everywhere That Mary Went ('93) ☆
Rita Morrone Hamilton
❑ ❑ 1 - Running from the Law ('95)

SEDLEY, Kate 🅿
Roger the Chapman
❑ ❑ 1 - Death and the Chapman ('91)
❑ ❑ 2 - The Plymouth Cloak ('92)
❑ ❑ 3 - The Weaver's Tale ('93)
❑ ❑ 4 - The Hanged Man ('93)
❑ ❑ 5 - The Holy Innocents ('94)

SHAFFER, Louise
Angie DaVito
❑ ❑ 1 - All My Suspects ('94)
❑ ❑ 2 - Talked to Death ('95)

SHAH, Diane K.
Paris Chandler
❑ ❑ 1 - As Crime Goes By ('90)
❑ ❑ 2 - Dying Cheek to Cheek ('92)

SHANKMAN, Sarah
Samantha Adams
❑ ❑ 1 - First Kill All the Lawyers ('88)
❑ ❑ 2 - Then Hang All the Liars ('89)
❑ ❑ 3 - Now Let's Talk of Graves ('90)
❑ ❑ 4 - She Walks in Beauty ('91)
❑ ❑ 5 - The King Is Dead ('92)
❑ ❑ 6 - He Was Her Man ('93)

SHANNON, Dell 🅿
Luis Mendoza
❑ ❑ 1 - Case Pending ('60) ☆
❑ ❑ 2 - The Ace of Spades ('60)
❑ ❑ 3 - Extra Kill ('61)
❑ ❑ 4 - Knave of Hearts ('62) ☆

SHELTON, Connie

Charlie Parker

SHEPHERD, Stella

Richard Montgomery

❑ ❑ 4 - A Lethal Fixation ('93)
❑ ❑ 5 - Nurse Dawes Is Dead ('94)
❑ ❑ 6 - Something in the Cellar ('95)

SHERIDAN, Juanita
Janice Cameron & Lily Wu
❑ ❑ 1 - The Chinese Chop ('49)
❑ ❑ 2 - The Kahuna Killer ('51)
❑ ❑ 3 - The Mamo Murders ('52)
[Britain-While the Coffin Waited]
❑ ❑ 4 - The Waikiki Widow ('53)

SHONE, Anna
Ulysses Finnegan Donaghue
❑ ❑ 1 - Mr. Donaghue Investigates ('95)

SHORT, Sharon Gwyn
Patricia Delaney
❑ ❑ 1 - Angel's Bidding ('94)
❑ ❑ 2 - Past Pretense ('94)
❑ ❑ 3 - The Death We Share ('95)

SIBLEY, Celestine
Kate Kincaid Mulcay
❑ ❑ 1 - The Malignant Heart ('58)
❑ ❑ 2 - Ah, Sweet Mystery ('91)
❑ ❑ 3 - Straight as an Arrow ('92)
❑ ❑ 4 - Dire Happenings at Scratch Ankle ('93)
❑ ❑ 5 - A Plague of Kinfolks ('95)

SILVA, Linda Kay
Delta Stevens
❑ ❑ 1 - Taken by Storm ('91)
❑ ❑ 2 - Storm Shelter ('93)
❑ ❑ 3 - Weathering the Storm ('94)
❑ ❑ 4 - Storm Front ('95)

SIMONSON, Sheila
Lark Dailey
❑ ❑ 1 - Larkspur ('90)
❑ ❑ 2 - Skylark ('92)
❑ ❑ 3 - Mudlark ('93)

 Who is the banking sleuth of Wall Street, featured in more than 20 financial mysteries?

SIMPSON, Dorothy
Luke Thanet
- ❏ ❏ 1 - The Night She Died ('81)
- ❏ ❏ 2 - Six Feet Under ('82)
- ❏ ❏ 3 - Puppet for a Corpse ('83)
- ❏ ❏ 4 - Close Her Eyes ('84)
- ❏ ❏ 5 - Last Seen Alive ('85) ★
- ❏ ❏ 6 - Dead on Arrival ('86)
- ❏ ❏ 7 - Element of Doubt ('87)
- ❏ ❏ 8 - Suspicious Death ('88)
- ❏ ❏ 9 - Dead by Morning ('89)
- ❏ ❏ 10 - Doomed to Die ('91)
- ❏ ❏ 11 - Wake Her Dead ('92)
- ❏ ❏ 12 - No Laughing Matter ('93)
- ❏ ❏ 13 - A Day for Dying ('95)

SIMS, L. V.
Dixie T. Struthers
- ❏ ❏ 1 - Murder Is Only Skin Deep ('87)
- ❏ ❏ 2 - Death Is a Family Affair ('87)
- ❏ ❏ 3 - To Sleep, Perchance to Kill ('88)

SINGER, Shelley
Barrett Lake
- ❏ ❏ 1 - Following Jane ('93)
- ❏ ❏ 2 - Picture of David ('93)
- ❏ ❏ 3 - Searching for Sara ('94)
- ❏ ❏ 4 - Interview with Mattie ('95)
- ❏ ❏ 5 - Anthony's Tattoo ('96)
Jake Samson & Rosie Vicente
- ❏ ❏ 1 - Samson's Deal ('83)
- ❏ ❏ 2 - Free Draw ('84)
- ❏ ❏ 3 - Full House ('86)
- ❏ ❏ 4 - Spit in the Ocean ('87)
- ❏ ❏ 5 - Suicide King ('88)

SJOWALL, Maj & Per Wahloo
Martin Beck
- ❏ ❏ 1 - Roseanna ('67)
- ❏ ❏ 2 - The Man on the Balcony ('68)
- ❏ ❏ 3 - The Man Who Went Up in Smoke ('69)
- ❏ ❏ 4 - The Laughing Policeman ('70) ★
- ❏ ❏ 5 - Murder at the Savoy ('71)
- ❏ ❏ 6 - The Fire Engine That Disappeared ('71)
- ❏ ❏ 7 - The Abominable Man ('72)

❑ ❑ 8 - The Locked Room ('73)
❑ ❑ 9 - Cop Killer ('75)
❑ ❑ 10 - The Terrorists ('76)

SKOM, Edith
Elizabeth Austin
❑ ❑ 1 - The Mark Twain Murders ('89) ☆ ☆ ☆
❑ ❑ 2 - The George Eliot Murder ('95)

SLOVO, Gillian
Kate Baeier
❑ ❑ 1 - Morbid Symptoms ('84)
❑ ❑ 2 - Death Comes Staccato ('87)
❑ ❑ 3 - Death by Analysis ('88)
❑ ❑ 4 - Catnap ('94)
❑ ❑ 5 - Close Call ('95)

SMITH, April
Ana Grey
❑ ❑ 1 - North of Montana ('94)

SMITH, Barbara Burnett
Jolie Wyatt
❑ ❑ 1 - Writers of the Purple Sage ('94) ☆
❑ ❑ 2 - Dust Devils of the Purple Sage ('95)
❑ ❑ 3 - Celebration in Purple Sage ('96)

SMITH, Evelyn E.
Susan Melville
❑ ❑ 1 - Miss Melville Regrets ('86)
❑ ❑ 2 - Miss Melville Returns ('87)
❑ ❑ 3 - Miss Melville's Revenge ('89)
❑ ❑ 4 - Miss Melville Rides a Tiger ('91)
❑ ❑ 5 - Miss Melville Runs for Cover ('95)

SMITH, J. C. S. 🅿
Quentin Jacoby
❑ ❑ 1 - Jacoby's First Case ('80)
❑ ❑ 2 - Nightcap ('84)

SMITH, Janet L.
Annie MacPherson
❑ ❑ 1 - Sea of Troubles ('90) ☆
❑ ❑ 2 - Practice to Deceive ('92)
❑ ❑ 3 - A Vintage Murder ('94)

SMITH, Joan G.
Cassie Newton
- ❏ ❏ 1 - Capriccio ('89)
- ❏ ❏ 2 - A Brush with Death ('90)

SMITH, Joan
Loretta Lawson
- ❏ ❏ 1 - A Masculine Ending ('87)
- ❏ ❏ 2 - Why Aren't They Screaming ('88)
- ❏ ❏ 3 - Don't Leave Me This Way ('90)
- ❏ ❏ 4 - What Men Say ('93)
- ❏ ❏ 5 - Full Stop ('95)

SMITH, Julie
Paul MacDonald
- ❏ ❏ 1 - True-Life Adventure ('85)
- ❏ ❏ 2 - Huckleberry Fiend ('87)
Rebecca Schwartz
- ❏ ❏ 1 - Death Turns a Trick ('82)
- ❏ ❏ 2 - The Sourdough Wars ('84)
- ❏ ❏ 3 - Tourist Trap ('86)
- ❏ ❏ 4 - Dead in the Water ('91)
- ❏ ❏ 5 - Other People's Skeletons ('93)
Skip Langdon
- ❏ ❏ 1 - New Orleans Mourning ('90) ★
- ❏ ❏ 2 - The Axeman's Jazz ('91)
- ❏ ❏ 3 - Jazz Funeral ('93)
- ❏ ❏ 4 - New Orleans Beat ('94)
- ❏ ❏ 5 - House of Blues ('95)

SPRING, Michelle
Laura Principal
- ❏ ❏ 1 - Every Breath You Take ('94) ☆ ☆
- ❏ ❏ 2 - Running for Shelter ('95)

SPRINKLE, Patricia H.
Sheila Travis
- ❏ ❏ 1 - Murder at Markham ('88)
- ❏ ❏ 2 - Murder in the Charleston Manner ('90)
- ❏ ❏ 3 - Murder on Peachtree Street ('91)
- ❏ ❏ 4 - Somebody's Dead in Snellville ('92)
- ❏ ❏ 5 - Death of a Dunwoody Matron ('93)
- ❏ ❏ 6 - A Mystery Bred in Buckhead ('94)
- ❏ ❏ 7 - Deadly Secrets on the St. Johns ('95)

SQUIRE, Elizabeth Daniels
Peaches Dann
- ❏ ❏ 1 - Who Killed What's-Her-Name? ('94)
- ❏ ❏ 2 - Remember the Alibi ('94)
- ❏ ❏ 3 - Memory Can Be Murder ('95)

STABENOW, Dana
Kate Shugak
- ❏ ❏ 1 - A Cold Day for Murder ('92) ★
- ❏ ❏ 2 - A Fatal Thaw ('93)
- ❏ ❏ 3 - Dead in the Water ('93)
- ❏ ❏ 4 - A Cold-Blooded Business ('94)
- ❏ ❏ 5 - Play with Fire ('95)

STACEY, Susannah 🄿
Robert Bone
- ❏ ❏ 1 - Goodbye Nanny Gray ('87) ☆
- ❏ ❏ 2 - A Knife at the Opera ('88)
- ❏ ❏ 3 - Body of Opinion ('88)
- ❏ ❏ 4 - Grave Responsibility ('90)
- ❏ ❏ 5 - The Late Lady ('92)
- ❏ ❏ 6 - Bone Idle ('93)
- ❏ ❏ 7 - Dead Serious ('95)

STALLWOOD, Veronica
Kate Ivory
- ❏ ❏ 1 - Death and the Oxford Box ('93)
- ❏ ❏ 2 - Oxford Exit ('95)
- ❏ ❏ 3 - Oxford Mourning ('96)

STEIN, Triss
Kay Engles
- ❏ ❏ 1 - Murder at the Class Reunion ('93)

STEINBERG, Janice
Margo Simon
- ❏ ❏ 1 - Death of a Postmodernist ('95)
- ❏ ❏ 2 - Death Crosses the Border ('95)

STEINER, Susan
Alex Winter
- ❏ ❏ 1 - Murder on Her Mind ('91)
- ❏ ❏ 2 - Library: No Murder Aloud ('93)

STEVENS, Serita
Fanny Zindel
❑ ❑ 1 - Red Sea, Dead Sea ('91)
❑ ❑ 2 - Bagels for Tea ('93)

SUCHER, Dorothy
Sabina Swift
❑ ❑ 1 - Dead Men Don't Give Seminars ('88) ☆
❑ ❑ 2 - Dead Men Don't Marry ('89)

SULLIVAN, Winona
Sister Cecile Buddenbrooks
❑ ❑ 1 - A Sudden Death at the Norfolk Cafe ('93) ★

SUMNER, Penny
Victoria Cross
❑ ❑ 1 - The End of April ('92)
❑ ❑ 2 - Crosswords ('95)

T

TAYLOR, Elizabeth Atwood
Maggie Elliott
❑ ❑ 1 - The Cable Car Murder ('81)
❑ ❑ 2 - Murder at Vassar ('87)
❑ ❑ 3 - The Northwest Murders ('92)

TAYLOR, Jean
Maggie Garrett
❑ ❑ 1 - We Know Where You Live ('95)
❑ ❑ 2 - The Last of Her Lies ('96)

TAYLOR, L. A.
J. J. Jamison
❑ ❑ 1 - Only Half a Hoax ('84)
❑ ❑ 2 - Deadly Objectives ('85)
❑ ❑ 3 - Shed Light on Death ('85)
❑ ❑ 4 - A Murder Waiting to Happen ('89)

TAYLOR, Phoebe Atwood
Asey Mayo
❑ ❑ 1 - The Cape Cod Mystery ('31)
❑ ❑ 2 - Death Lights a Candle ('32)
❑ ❑ 3 - The Mystery of the Cape Cod Players ('33)
❑ ❑ 4 - The Mystery of the Cape Cod Tavern ('34)

❑ ❑ 5 - Sandbar Sinister ('34)
❑ ❑ 6 - The Tinkling Symbol ('35)
❑ ❑ 7 - Deathblow Hill ('35)
❑ ❑ 8 - The Crimson Patch ('36)
❑ ❑ 9 - Out of Order ('36)
❑ ❑ 10 - Figure Away ('37)
❑ ❑ 11 - Octagon House ('37)
❑ ❑ 12 - The Annulet of Gilt ('38)
❑ ❑ 13 - Banbury Bog ('38)
❑ ❑ 14 - Spring Harrowing ('39)
❑ ❑ 15 - The Deadly Sunshade ('40)
❑ ❑ 16 - The Criminal C.O.D. ('40)
❑ ❑ 17 - The Perennial Border ('41)
❑ ❑ 18 - Three Plots for Asey Mayo ('42)
❑ ❑ 19 - The Six Iron Spiders ('42)
❑ ❑ 20 - Going, Going, Gone ('43)
❑ ❑ 21 - Proof of the Pudding ('45)
❑ ❑ 22 - Punch with Care ('46)
❑ ❑ 23 - The Asey Mayo Trio ('46)
❑ ❑ 24 - Diplomatic Corpse ('51)

TELL, Dorothy
Poppy Dillworth
❑ ❑ 1 - Murder at Red Rook Ranch ('90)
❑ ❑ 2 - Wilderness Trek ('90)
❑ ❑ 3 - The Hallelujah Murders ('91)

TEY, Josephine 🄿
Alan Grant
❑ ❑ 1 - The Man in the Queue ('29)
❑ ❑ 2 - A Shilling for Candles ('36)
❑ ❑ 3 - The Franchise Affair ('49)
❑ ❑ 4 - To Love and Be Wise ('50)
❑ ❑ 5 - The Daughter of Time ('51)
❑ ❑ 6 - The Singing Sands ('52)

THOMPSON, Joyce
Frederika Bascomb
❑ ❑ 1 - Bones ('91)

THOMSON, June
Insp. Finch [Insp. Rudd in U.S.]
❑ ❑ 1 - Not One of Us ('71)
❑ ❑ 2 - Death Cap ('73)
❑ ❑ 3 - The Long Revenge ('74)
❑ ❑ 4 - Case Closed ('77)

THURLO, Aimee & David
Ella Clah

TILTON, Alice 🅿
Leonidas Witherall

TONE, Teona
Kyra Keaton

TORRIE, Malcolm 🅿
Timothy Herring

TRAVIS, Elizabeth
Ben & Carrie Porter
- ❏ ❏ 1 - Under the Influence ('89)
- ❏ ❏ 2 - Finders Keepers ('90)

TROCHECK, Kathy Hogan
Callahan Garrity
- ❏ ❏ 1 - Every Crooked Nanny ('92) ☆
- ❏ ❏ 2 - To Live and Die in Dixie ('93) ☆ ☆
- ❏ ❏ 3 - Homemade Sin ('94)
- ❏ ❏ 4 - Happy Never After ('95)

Truman Kicklighter
- ❏ ❏ 1 - Lickety Split ('96)

TRUMAN, Margaret
Mackenzie Smith & Annabel Reed
- ❏ ❏ 1 - Murder at the Kennedy Center ('89)
- ❏ ❏ 2 - Murder at the National Cathedral ('90)
- ❏ ❏ 3 - Murder at the Pentagon ('92)
- ❏ ❏ 4 - Murder on the Potomac ('94)
- ❏ ❏ 5 - Murder at the National Gallery ('95)

TUCKER, Kerry
Libby Kincaid
- ❏ ❏ 1 - Still Waters ('91)
- ❏ ❏ 2 - Cold Feet ('92)
- ❏ ❏ 3 - Death Echo ('93)
- ❏ ❏ 4 - Drift Away ('94)

TYRE, Peg
Kate Murray
- ❏ ❏ 1 - Strangers in the Night ('94)
- ❏ ❏ 2 - In the Midnight Hour ('95)

U

UHNAK, Dorothy
Christine Opara
- ❏ ❏ 1 - The Bait ('68) ★
- ❏ ❏ 2 - The Witness ('69)
- ❏ ❏ 3 - The Ledger ('70) ★

━━━━━━━━━━ ∨ ━━━━━━━━━━

VALENTINE, Deborah
Katharine Craig & Kevin Bryce
- ❏ ❏ 1 - Unorthodox Methods ('89)
- ❏ ❏ 2 - A Collector of Photographs ('89) ☆ ☆
- ❏ ❏ 3 - Fine Distinctions ('91) ☆

VAN GIESON, Judith
Neil Hamel
- ❏ ❏ 1 - North of the Border ('88)
- ❏ ❏ 2 - Raptor ('90)
- ❏ ❏ 3 - The Other Side of Death ('91)
- ❏ ❏ 4 - The Wolf Path ('92)
- ❏ ❏ 5 - The Lies that Bind ('93) ☆
- ❏ ❏ 6 - Parrot Blues ('95)

VENNING, Michael 🅿
Melville Fairr
- ❏ ❏ 1 - The Man Who Slept All Day ('42)
- ❏ ❏ 2 - Murder Through the Looking Glass ('43)
- ❏ ❏ 3 - Jethro Hammer ('44)

VLASOPOLOS, Anca
Sharon Dair
- ❏ ❏ 1 - Missing Members ('90)

━━━━━━━━━━ W ━━━━━━━━━━

WAKEFIELD, Hannah 🅿
Dee Street
- ❏ ❏ 1 - The Price You Pay ('87)
- ❏ ❏ 2 - A Woman's Own Mystery ('90)
  [Britain-A February Mourning]

WALKER, Mary Willis
Kate Driscoll
- ❏ ❏ 1 - Zero at the Bone ('91) ★ ★ ☆
Molly Cates
- ❏ ❏ 1 - The Red Scream ('94) ★
- ❏ ❏ 2 - Under the Beetle's Cellar ('95)

WALLACE, Marilyn
Jay Goldstein & Carlos Cruz
- ❏ ❏ 1 - A Case of Loyalties ('86) ★
- ❏ ❏ 2 - Primary Target ('88) ☆
- ❏ ❏ 3 - A Single Stone ('91) ☆

WALLACE, Patricia
Sydney Bryant
- ❏ ❏ 1 - Small Favors ('88)
- ❏ ❏ 2 - Deadly Grounds ('89)
- ❏ ❏ 3 - Blood Lies ('91)
- ❏ ❏ 4 - Deadly Devotion ('94) ☆
- ❏ ❏ 5 - Dark Intent ('95)

WALLINGFORD, Lee
Ginny Trask & Frank Carver
- ❏ ❏ 1 - Cold Tracks ('91)
- ❏ ❏ 2 - Clear Cut Murder ('93)

WALSH, Jill Paton
Imogen Quy
- ❏ ❏ 1 - The Wyndham Case ('93)
- ❏ ❏ 2 - A Piece of Justice ('95)

WALTCH, Lilla M.
Lisa Davis
- ❏ ❏ 1 - The Third Victim ('87)
- ❏ ❏ 2 - Fearful Symmetry ('88)

WARMBOLD, Jean
Sarah Calloway
- ❏ ❏ 1 - June Mail ('86)
- ❏ ❏ 2 - The White Hand ('88)
- ❏ ❏ 3 - The Third Way ('89)

WARNER, Mignon
Edwina Charles
- ❏ ❏ 1 - A Medium for Murder ('76)
  [Britain-A Nice Way to Die]
- ❏ ❏ 2 - The Tarot Murders ('78)
- ❏ ❏ 3 - Death in Time ('80)
- ❏ ❏ 4 - The Girl Who Was Clairvoyant ('82)
- ❏ ❏ 5 - Devil's Knell ('83)
- ❏ ❏ 6 - Illusion ('84)
- ❏ ❏ 7 - Speak No Evil ('85)

WATSON, Clarissa
Persis Willum
- ☐ ☐ 1 - The Fourth Stage of Gainsborough Brown ('77)
- ☐ ☐ 2 - The Bishop in the Back Seat ('80)
- ☐ ☐ 3 - Runaway ('85)
- ☐ ☐ 4 - Last Plane from Nice ('88)
- ☐ ☐ 5 - Somebody Killed the Messenger ('88)

WEBB, Martha G. 🅟
Tommy Inman
- ☐ ☐ 1 - A White Male Running ('85)
- ☐ ☐ 2 - Even Cops' Daughters ('86)

WEIR, Charlene
Susan Wren
- ☐ ☐ 1 - The Winter Widow ('92) ★ ☆
- ☐ ☐ 2 - Consider the Crows ('93) ☆
- ☐ ☐ 3 - Family Medicine ('95)

WELCH, Pat
Helen Black
- ☐ ☐ 1 - Murder by the Book ('90)
- ☐ ☐ 2 - Still Waters ('92)
- ☐ ☐ 3 - A Proper Burial ('93)
- ☐ ☐ 4 - Open House ('95)

WELLS, Carolyn
Fleming Stone
- ☐ ☐ 1 - The Clue ('09)
- ☐ ☐ 2 - The Gold Bag ('11)
- ☐ ☐ 3 - A Chain of Evidence ('12)
- ☐ ☐ 4 - The Maxwell Mystery ('13)
- ☐ ☐ 5 - Anybody But Anne ('14)
- ☐ ☐ 6 - The White Alley ('15)
- ☐ ☐ 7 - The Curved Blades ('16)
- ☐ ☐ 8 - The Mark of Cain ('17)
- ☐ ☐ 9 - Vicky Van ('18)
- ☐ ☐ 10 - The Diamond Pin ('19)
- ☐ ☐ 11 - Raspberry Jam ('20)
- ☐ ☐ 12 - The Mystery of the Sycamore ('21)
- ☐ ☐ 13 - The Mystery Girl ('22)
- ☐ ☐ 14 - Feathers Left Around ('23)
- ☐ ☐ 15 - Spooky Hollow ('23)
- ☐ ☐ 16 - The Furthest Fury ('24)
- ☐ ☐ 17 - Prilligirl ('24)

❏ ❏ 18 - Anything But the Truth ('25)
❏ ❏ 19 - The Daughter of the House ('25)
❏ ❏ 20 - The Bronze Hand ('26)
❏ ❏ 21 - The Red-Haired Girl ('26)
❏ ❏ 22 - All at Sea ('27)
❏ ❏ 23 - Where's Emily ('27)
❏ ❏ 24 - The Crime in the Crypt ('28)
❏ ❏ 25 - The Tannahill Tangle ('28)
❏ ❏ 26 - The Tapestry Room Murder ('29)
❏ ❏ 27 - Triple Murder ('29)
❏ ❏ 28 - The Doomed Five ('30)
❏ ❏ 29 - The Ghosts' High Noon ('30)
❏ ❏ 30 - Horror House ('31)
❏ ❏ 31 - The Umbrella Murder ('31)
❏ ❏ 32 - Fuller's Earth ('32)
❏ ❏ 33 - The Roll-Top Desk Mystery ('32)
❏ ❏ 34 - The Broken O ('33)
❏ ❏ 35 - The Clue of the Eyelash ('33)
❏ ❏ 36 - The Master Murderer ('33)
❏ ❏ 37 - Eyes in the Wall ('34)
❏ ❏ 38 - The Visiting Villain ('34)
❏ ❏ 39 - For Goodness' Sake ('35)
❏ ❏ 40 - The Beautiful Derelict ('35)
❏ ❏ 41 - The Wooden Indian ('35)
❏ ❏ 42 - Money Musk ('36)
❏ ❏ 43 - The Huddle ('36)
❏ ❏ 44 - Murder in the Bookshop ('36)
❏ ❏ 45 - The Mystery of the Tarn ('37)
❏ ❏ 46 - In the Tiger's Cage ('36)
❏ ❏ 47 - The Radio Studio Murder ('37)
❏ ❏ 48 - Gilt-Edged Guilt ('38)
❏ ❏ 49 - The Killer ('38)
❏ ❏ 50 - The Missing Link ('38)
❏ ❏ 51 - Calling All Suspects ('39)
❏ ❏ 52 - Crime Tears On ('39)
❏ ❏ 53 - The Importance of Being Murdered ('39)
❏ ❏ 54 - Crime Incarnate ('40)
❏ ❏ 55 - Devil's Work ('40)
❏ ❏ 56 - Murder on Parade ('40)
❏ ❏ 57 - Murder Plus ('40)
❏ ❏ 58 - The Black Night Murders ('41)
❏ ❏ 59 - Murder at the Casino ('41)
❏ ❏ 60 - Murder Will In ('42)
❏ ❏ 61 - Who Killed Caldwell? ('42)

Kenneth Carlisle
- ❏ ❏ 1 - Sleeping Dogs ('29)
- ❏ ❏ 2 - The Doorstep Murders ('30)
- ❏ ❏ 3 - The Skeleton at the Feast ('31)

Pennington Wise
- ❏ ❏ 1 - The Room with the Tassels ('18)
- ❏ ❏ 2 - The Man Who Fell Through the Earth ('19)
- ❏ ❏ 3 - In the Onyx Lobby ('20)
- ❏ ❏ 4 - The Come-Back ('21)
- ❏ ❏ 5 - The Luminous Face ('21)
- ❏ ❏ 6 - The Vanishing of Betty Varian ('22)
- ❏ ❏ 7 - The Affair at Flower Acres ('23)
- ❏ ❏ 8 - Wheels Within Wheels ('23)

WELLS, Tobias ▣

Knute Severson
- ❏ ❏ 1 - A Matter of Love and Death ('66)
- ❏ ❏ 2 - Dead by the Light of the Moon ('67)
- ❏ ❏ 3 - What Should You Know of Dying? ('67)
- ❏ ❏ 4 - Murder Most Fouled Up ('68)
- ❏ ❏ 5 - The Young Can Die Protesting ('69)
- ❏ ❏ 6 - Die Quickly, Dear Mother ('69)
- ❏ ❏ 7 - Dinky Died ('70)
- ❏ ❏ 8 - The Foo Dog ('71) [Britain-The Lotus Affair]
- ❏ ❏ 9 - What To Do Until the Undertaker Comes ('71)
- ❏ ❏ 10 - A Die in the Country ('72)
- ❏ ❏ 11 - How to Kill a Man ('72)
- ❏ ❏ 12 - Brenda's Murder ('73)
- ❏ ❏ 13 - Have Mercy Upon Us ('74)
- ❏ ❏ 14 - Hark, Hark, the Watchdogs Bark ('75)
- ❏ ❏ 15 - A Creature Was Stirring ('77)
- ❏ ❏ 16 - Of Graves, Worms and Epitaphs ('88)

WENDER, Theodora

Glad Gold & Alden Chase
- ❏ ❏ 1 - Knight Must Fall ('85)
- ❏ ❏ 2 - Murder Gets a Degree ('86)

WENTWORTH, Patricia ▣

Insp. Ernest Lamb
- ❏ ❏ 1 - The Blind Side ('39)
- ❏ ❏ 2 - Pursuit of a Parcel ('42)

Maud Silver
- ❏ ❏ 1 - Grey Mask ('28)
- ❏ ❏ 2 - The Case Is Closed ('37)

❏ ❏ 3 - Lonesome Road ('39)
❏ ❏ 4 - In the Balance ('41)
        [Britain-Danger Point]
❏ ❏ 5 - The Chinese Shawl ('43)
❏ ❏ 6 - Miss Silver Deals in Death ('43)
        [Britain-Miss S. Intervenes]
❏ ❏ 7 - The Clock Strikes Twelve ('44)
❏ ❏ 8 - The Key ('44)
❏ ❏ 9 - She Came Back ('45)
        [Britain-The Traveller Returns]
❏ ❏ 10 - Pilgrim's Rest ('46)
        [APA-Dark Threat]
❏ ❏ 11 - Latter End ('47)
❏ ❏ 12 - Wicked Uncle ('47)
        [Britain-The Spotlight]
❏ ❏ 13 - The Eternity Ring ('48)
❏ ❏ 14 - The Case of William Smith ('48)
❏ ❏ 15 - Miss Silver Comes to Stay ('49)
❏ ❏ 16 - The Catherine Wheel ('49)
❏ ❏ 17 - Through the Wall ('50)
❏ ❏ 18 - The Brading Collection ('50)
        [APA-Mr. Brading's Collection]
❏ ❏ 19 - The Ivory Dagger ('51)
❏ ❏ 20 - Anna, Where Are You? ('51)
        [APA-Death at Deep End]
❏ ❏ 21 - The Watersplash ('51)
❏ ❏ 22 - Ladies' Bane ('52)
❏ ❏ 23 - Out of the Past ('53)
❏ ❏ 24 - Vanishing Point ('53)
❏ ❏ 25 - The Silent Pool ('54)
❏ ❏ 26 - The Benevent Treasure ('54)
❏ ❏ 27 - The Listening Eye ('55)
❏ ❏ 28 - The Gazebo ('56)
        [APA-The Summerhouse]
❏ ❏ 29 - The Fingerprint ('56)
❏ ❏ 30 - Poison in the Pen ('57)
❏ ❏ 31 - The Alington Inheritance ('58)
❏ ❏ 32 - The Girl in the Cellar ('61)

WESLEY, Valerie Wilson

Tamara Hayle

❏ ❏ 1 - When Death Comes Stealing ('94) ☆
❏ ❏ 2 - Devil's Gonna Get Him ('95)

WEST, Chassie

Leigh Ann Warren
- ❑ ❑ 1 - Sunrise ('94) ☆

WESTON, Carolyn

Casey Kellog & Al Krug
- ❑ ❑ 1 - Poor, Poor Ophelia ('72)
- ❑ ❑ 2 - Susannah Screaming ('75)
- ❑ ❑ 3 - Rouse the Demon ('76)

WHEAT, Carolyn

Cass Jameson
- ❑ ❑ 1 - Dead Man's Thoughts ('83) ☆
- ❑ ❑ 2 - Where Nobody Dies ('86)
- ❑ ❑ 3 - Fresh Kills ('95)

WHITE, Gloria

Ronnie Ventana
- ❑ ❑ 1 - Murder on the Run ('91) ☆
- ❑ ❑ 2 - Money to Burn ('93)
- ❑ ❑ 3 - Charged with Guilt ('95)

WHITE, Teri

Spaceman Kowalski & Blue Maguire
- ❑ ❑ 1 - Bleeding Hearts ('84)
- ❑ ❑ 2 - Tightrope ('86)

WHITNEY, Polly

Mary "Ike" Tygart & "Abby" Abagnarro
- ❑ ❑ 1 - Until Death ('94) ☆
- ❑ ❑ 2 - Until the End of Time ('95)
- ❑ ❑ 3 - Until it Hurts ('96)

WILHELM, Kate

Barbara Holloway
- ❑ ❑ 1 - Death Qualified ('91)
- ❑ ❑ 2 - The Best Defense ('94)

Charlie Meiklejohn & Constance Leidl
- ❑ ❑ 1 - The Hamlet Trap ('87)
- ❑ ❑ 2 - The Dark Door ('88)
- ❑ ❑ 3 - Smart House ('89)
- ❑ ❑ 4 - Sweet, Sweet Poison ('90)
- ❑ ❑ 5 - Seven Kinds of Death ('92)
- ❑ ❑ 6 - A Flush of Shadows [5 novellas] ('95)

Sarah Drexler
- ❑ ❑ 1 - Justice for Some ('93)

WILSON, Barbara

Cassandra Reilly
- ❏ ❏ 1 - Gaudi Afternoon ('90) ★
- ❏ ❏ 2 - Trouble in Transylvania ('93)

Pam Nilsen
- ❏ ❏ 1 - Murder in the Collective ('84)
- ❏ ❏ 2 - Sisters of the Road ('86)
- ❏ ❏ 3 - The Dog Collar Murders ('89)

WILSON, Karen Ann

Samantha Holt
- ❏ ❏ 1 - Eight Dogs Flying ('94)
- ❏ ❏ 2 - Copy Cat Crimes ('95)

WILTZ, Chris

Neal Rafferty
- ❏ ❏ 1 - The Killing Circle ('81)
- ❏ ❏ 2 - A Diamond Before You Die ('87)
- ❏ ❏ 3 - The Emerald Lizard ('91)

WINGATE, Ann

Mark Shigata
- ❏ ❏ 1 - Death by Deception ('88)
- ❏ ❏ 2 - The Eye of Anna ('89)
- ❏ ❏ 3 - The Buzzards Must Also Be Fed ('91)
- ❏ ❏ 4 - Exception to Murder ('92)
- ❏ ❏ 5 - Yakuza, Go Home! ('93)

WINGS, Mary P

Emma Victor
- ❏ ❏ 1 - She Came Too Late ('87)
- ❏ ❏ 2 - She Came in a Flash ('90)
- ❏ ❏ 3 - She Came by the Book ('95)

WINSLOW, Pauline Glen

Merlin Capricorn
- ❏ ❏ 1 - Death of an Angel ('75)
- ❏ ❏ 2 - The Brandenburg Hotel ('76)
- ❏ ❏ 3 - The Witch Hill Murder ('77)
- ❏ ❏ 4 - Copper Gold ('78)
  [Britain-Coppergold]
- ❏ ❏ 5 - The Counsellor Heart ('80)
  [APA-Sister Death]
- ❏ ❏ 6 - The Rockefeller Gift ('82)

WOLFE, Susan
Sarah Nelson
❑ ❑ 1 - The Last Billable Hour ('89) ★

WOLZIEN, Valerie
Josie Pigeon
❑ ❑ 1 - Shore to Die ('96)
Susan Henshaw
❑ ❑ 1 - Murder at the PTA Luncheon ('87)
❑ ❑ 2 - The Fortieth Birthday Body ('89)
❑ ❑ 3 - We Wish You a Merry Murder ('91)
❑ ❑ 4 - All Hallow's Evil ('92)
❑ ❑ 5 - An Old Faithful Murder ('92)
❑ ❑ 6 - A Star-Spangled Murder ('93)
❑ ❑ 7 - A Good Year for a Corpse ('94)
❑ ❑ 8 - Tis the Season To Be Murdered ('94)
❑ ❑ 9 - Remodeled to Death ('95)
❑ ❑ 10 - Elected to Die ('96)

WOODS, Sara 🅿
Antony Maitland
❑ ❑ 1 - Bloody Instructions ('62)
❑ ❑ 2 - Malice Domestic ('62)
❑ ❑ 3 - The Taste of Fears ('63)
　　　　[APA-The Third Encounter]
❑ ❑ 4 - Error of the Moon ('63)
❑ ❑ 5 - Trusted Like the Fox ('64)
❑ ❑ 6 - This Little Measure ('64)
❑ ❑ 7 - The Windy Side of the Law ('65)
❑ ❑ 8 - Though I Know She Lies ('65)
❑ ❑ 9 - Enter Certain Murderers ('66)
❑ ❑ 10 - Let's Choose Executors ('66)
❑ ❑ 11 - The Case Is Altered ('67)
❑ ❑ 12 - And Shame the Devil ('67)
❑ ❑ 13 - Knives Have Edges ('68)
❑ ❑ 14 - Past Praying For ('68)
❑ ❑ 15 - Tarry and Be Hanged ('69)
❑ ❑ 16 - An Improbable Fiction ('70)
❑ ❑ 17 - Serpent's Tooth ('71)
❑ ❑ 18 - The Knavish Crows ('71)
❑ ❑ 19 - They Love Not Poison [prequel] ('72)
❑ ❑ 20 - Yet She Must Die ('73)
❑ ❑ 21 - Enter the Corpse ('73)
❑ ❑ 22 - Done to Death ('74)
❑ ❑ 23 - A Show of Violence ('75)

❏ ❏ 24 - My Life Is Done ('76)
❏ ❏ 25 - The Law's Delay ('77)
❏ ❏ 26 - A Thief or Two ('77)
❏ ❏ 27 - Exit Murderer ('78)
❏ ❏ 28 - This Fatal Writ ('79)
❏ ❏ 29 - Proceed to Judgement ('79)
❏ ❏ 30 - They Stay for Death ('80)
❏ ❏ 31 - Weep for Her ('80)
❏ ❏ 32 - Dearest Enemy ('81)
❏ ❏ 33 - Cry Guilty ('81)
❏ ❏ 34 - Villains by Necessity ('82)
❏ ❏ 35 - Enter a Gentlewoman ('82)
❏ ❏ 36 - Most Grievous Murder ('82)
❏ ❏ 37 - The Lie Direct ('83)
❏ ❏ 38 - Call Back Yesterday ('83)
❏ ❏ 39 - Where Should He Die? ('83)
❏ ❏ 40 - The Bloody Book of Law ('84)
❏ ❏ 41 - Defy the Devil ('84)
❏ ❏ 42 - Murder's Out of Tune ('84)
❏ ❏ 43 - An Obscure Grave ('85)
❏ ❏ 44 - Away with Them to Prison ('85)
❏ ❏ 45 - Put Out the Light ('85)
❏ ❏ 46 - Nor Live So Long ('86)
❏ ❏ 47 - Most Deadly Hate ('86)
❏ ❏ 48 - Naked Villainy ('87)

WOODS, Sherryl
Amanda Roberts
❏ ❏ 1 - Reckless ('89)
❏ ❏ 2 - Body and Soul ('89)
❏ ❏ 3 - Stolen Moments ('90)
❏ ❏ 4 - Ties That Bind ('91)
❏ ❏ 5 - Bank on It ('93)
❏ ❏ 6 - Hide and Seek ('93)
❏ ❏ 7 - Wages of Sin ('94)
❏ ❏ 8 - Deadly Obsession ('95)
❏ ❏ 9 - White Lightning ('95)

Molly Dewitt
❏ ❏ 1 - Hot Property ('91)
❏ ❏ 2 - Hot Secret ('92)
❏ ❏ 3 - Hot Money ('93)
❏ ❏ 4 - Hot Schemes ('94)
❏ ❏ 5 - Hot Ticket ('95)

WREN, M. K. 🄿
Conan Flagg
- ❑ ❑ 1 - Curiosity Didn't Kill the Cat ('73)
- ❑ ❑ 2 - A Multitude of Sins ('75)
- ❑ ❑ 3 - Oh Bury Me Not ('77)
- ❑ ❑ 4 - Nothing's Certain But Death ('78)
- ❑ ❑ 5 - Seasons of Death ('81)
- ❑ ❑ 6 - Wake Up, Darlin' Corey ('84)
- ❑ ❑ 7 - Dead Matter ('93)
- ❑ ❑ 8 - King of the Mountain ('95)

WRIGHT, L. R. (Laurali)
Martin Karl Alberg
- ❑ ❑ 1 - The Suspect ('85) ★
- ❑ ❑ 2 - Sleep While I Sing ('86)
- ❑ ❑ 3 - A Chill Rain in January ('90) ★
- ❑ ❑ 4 - Fall from Grace ('91)
- ❑ ❑ 5 - Prized Possessions ('93)
- ❑ ❑ 6 - A Touch of Panic ('94) ☆
- ❑ ❑ 7 - Mother Love ('95)

𝒴

YARBRO, Chelsea Quinn
Charles Spotted Moon
- ❑ ❑ 1 - Ogilvie, Tallant and Moon ('76)
  [APA-Bad Medicine ('90)]
- ❑ ❑ 2 - Music When Sweet Voices Die ('79)
  [APA-False Notes ('90)]
- ❑ ❑ 3 - Poison Fruit ('91)
- ❑ ❑ 4 - Cat's Claw ('92)

YATES, Margaret Tayler
Anne "Davvie" Davenport McLean
- ❑ ❑ 1 - The Hush-Hush Murders ('37)
- ❑ ❑ 2 - Death Send a Cable ('39)
- ❑ ❑ 3 - Midway to Murder ('41)
- ❑ ❑ 4 - Murder by the Yard ('42)

YEAGER, Dorian
Elizabeth Will
- ❑ ❑ 1 - Murder Will Out ('94)
- ❑ ❑ 2 - Summer Will End ('95)

Z